Counseling Depressed Women

Counseling and Pastoral Theology

Andrew D. Lester, Series Editor

Counseling Depressed Women

Susan J. Dunlap

Westminster John Knox Press
Louisville, Kentucky

Scripture quotations from the New Revised Standard Version of the
Bible are copyright © 1989 by the Division of Christian Education of the
National Council of the Churches of Christ in the U.S.A.
and are used by permission.

Book design by Jennifer K. Cox
Cover design by Kevin Darst

First Edition
Published by Westminster John Knox Press
Louisville, Kentucky

This book is printed on acid-free paper that meets the
American National Standards Institute Z39.48 standard. ∞

PRINTED IN THE UNITED STATES OF AMERICA

97 98 99 00 01 02 03 04 05 06 — 10 9 8 7 6 5 4 3 2 1

Library of Congress Cataloging-in-Publication Data

Dunlap, Susan J., date.
    Counseling depressed women / Susan J. Dunlap. — 1st ed.
        p.   cm. — (Counseling and pastoral theology)
    Includes bibliographical references and index.
    ISBN 0-664-25667-8
    1. Depressed persons—Pastoral counseling of.   2. Women—Pastoral
counseling of.   3. Depression, Mental—Religious aspects—
Christianity.   I. Title.   II. Series.
BV4461.D86   1997
259'.425—dc21   97-14697

To Mary Buchanan Renshaw Leonard

whom I knew as
Polly
my mentor and friend

Contents

Foreword

Depression can be "a form of 'brain pain' that is practically unendurable," says Susan Dunlap, one in which "faith dies, hope withers, love is impossible." Compassion for those who suffer from this debilitating illness demands a creative response from pastoral caregivers. Using the latest research from a variety of disciplines, Dunlap develops a holistic model that incorporates biological, psychological, and sociological contributions to depression. The inadequacy of theories that discount any one of these perspectives is clearly demonstrated. This inclusive model leads her to reject concepts that rigidly identify various kinds of depression and argues for a "lifespan perspective."

Women become depressed at twice the rate of men. Why? Dunlap's central perspective is on the lack of power, both the reality of cultural powerlessness and the resultant psychological belief system. After discussing the concept of power, she explores five themes closely associated with women's depression. (1) The social position of women in our patriarchal culture contributes to the powerlessness so evident in depression. (2) Loss of self, the silencing of self, or what Dunlap calls the "eclipsed self," resulting from the multiple discounts that attend to women's socialization, also puts women at risk. (3) What happens to women in intimate relationships is another unique factor that makes them more vulnerable to depression, not because of women's pathological dependency, but because of the difficulty of establishing meaningful connections in our culture, particularly with men. (4) The objectification of women's bodies is another contributor to loss of self, anger, and, of course, depression. (5) Women tend to fear the powerful emotion of anger. This fear and the lack of power to effect change results in frustration and the ineffective use of anger, which contributes to women's depression.

Dunlap chooses cognitive therapy as the strategy of choice for pastoral caregivers because the assumptions of this theory about personhood match her biopsychosocial model. She discusses this model in an early chapter and then uses clinical material throughout to demonstrate this mode of intervention. These clinical illustrations bring her concepts to life.

Theological concepts are integrally woven into Dunlap's work. She describes the theological questions raised by the human experience of depression from the perspective of the sufferer, the caregiver, and the scholar, exploring the differences in theological questions and answers for each.

xii   *Foreword*

The last chapter identifies hope as the primary antidote to depression. Dunlap's pastoral theology focuses on the power of hope within the Christian narrative to facilitate deliverance from this adversary, particularly for women. This book provides excellent guidance for us as we learn to recognize, understand, and offer effective intervention.

The *Counseling and Pastoral Theology* Series

The purpose of this series is to address clinical issues that arise among particular populations currently neglected in the literature on pastoral care and counseling (women in lesbian relationships, African-American couples, adolescents under stress, women who are depressed, survivors of sexual abuse, adult adoptees, persons with terminal illness, and couples experiencing infertility). This series is committed to enhance both the theoretical base and the clinical expertise of pastoral caregivers by providing a pastoral theological paradigm that will inform both assessment and intervention with persons in these specific populations.

Many books on pastoral care and counseling are more carefully informed by the behavioral and social sciences than by classical theological disciplines. Pastoral care and counseling specialists have been criticized for ignoring our theological heritage, challenged to reevaluate our idolization of psychology and to claim our unique perspectives on the human predicament. The discipline of pastoral theology has made significant strides in the last decade. The Society for Pastoral Theology was formed in 1985 and now publishes *The Journal of Pastoral Theology.*

Pastoral theology grows out of data gathered from at least three sources: (1) revelation about the human condition uncovered by the social and behavioral sciences, (2) wisdom from the classical theological disciplines, and (3) insight garnered from reflection on the pastoral ministry event. The development of pastoral theology grows out of the dialogue between these three perspectives, each perspective enabled to ask questions of, challenge, and critique the other perspectives.

Each author is clinically experienced and academically prepared to write about the particular population with which she or he is personally concerned and professionally involved. Each author develops a "constructive pastoral theology," resulting in the theological frame of reference that provides the unique perspective from which a pastoral person approaches both assessment and intervention. This constructive pastoral theology will enable clinically trained pastors and pastoral care specialists (pastoral counselors, chaplains, Clinical Pastoral Education supervisors) to creatively participate in pastoral relationships that effectively enable healing, sustaining, guiding, reconciling, and liberating.

Though the focus will be on offering pastoral care and counseling to individuals, couples, and families, each author is cognizant of the interaction between individuals and their environment. These books will consider the effects of larger systems—from family of origin to cultural constructs. Each author will use case material from her or his clinical pastoral ministry to focus the reader's attention on the issues faced by the particular population as viewed from the pastoral theological paradigm.

My thanks to colleagues who faithfully served on the Advisory Committee and expended many hours of creative work to ensure that this series would make a substantial contribution: Bonnie Miller-McLemore (1992–1996), Nancy Ramsay (1992–1996), Han van den Blink (1992–1994), Larry Kent Graham (1994–1996), and Linda Kirkland-Harris (1994–1996).

Andrew D. Lester
Brite Divinity School

Acknowledgments

Because this book began as a dissertation, I want to begin by thanking the members of my dissertation committee. Laura Marder guided my learning of the art of psychotherapy in a gentle and collegial way. Mark Taylor offered clear and rigorous thinking about my project, as well as assurance that it was a valuable contribution to the field. Donald Capps, my advisor, has consistently been a great support. His iconoclasm, integrity, encouragement for my intellectual curiosity, and prompt feedback have been invaluable.

The readers of this book have offered extraordinarily helpful suggestions: Gloria Albrecht, Donald Capps, Mary McClintock Fulkerson, Elizabeth Maxwell, and Christie Cozad Neuger. I have benefited greatly from their wisdom and experience as well as their careful attention to this manuscript.

I also want to thank some of my earlier teachers: John Bachman, Tom Raitt, George Stroup, and John Mulder. I am especially grateful to my former teacher Mary McClintock Fulkerson, who opened a new theological world to me, and who, as a colleague, serves as a model of the kind of scholar I would like to be.

One particular group of people has endured in its encouragement: the congregation of Dickey Memorial Presbyterian Church, whom I served as pastor. The congregation has provided continuing friendship and warmth as well as financial aid for my studies. This book is dedicated to Polly Leonard, Dickey Memorial's Clerk of Session for most of the time I was there. She was a courageous, compassionate, committed, and visionary woman, and she has left an indelible mark on my life.

Don Strauss has been an immeasurably important mentor, priest, friend, and storyteller. For the doors he opened and the challenges to take risks and live passionately, I am deeply grateful.

Harold and Jean, my parents, and Paul and Kent, my brothers, have given me great love and companionship, shared their curiosity about things holy and human, nature and culture, and the wonder of ideas and discoveries of many sorts. They have intimately shaped me as a scholar.

Finally, I want to thank Prasad, my husband, whose love and steadfast presence sustained me throughout the writing and rewriting of this book. He brought coffee, charted the phases of this book's completion, and provided unfailing and delightful humor. He has shown extraordinary commitment to my work, and I will always be grateful.

Introduction

Depression can be a form of "brain pain" that is practically unendurable. For many who have been depressed, not only is the face of God eclipsed, but their own souls are in eclipse. Faith dies, hope withers, love is impossible. The sense of isolation and self-loathing is overwhelming. In fact, many sufferers from depression do conclude that the pain is unbearable, and end their own lives. Freud tells us that depression involves "an overcoming of the instinct which compels every living thing to cling to life."[1] The experience of depression has been called "a life that is unlivable, heavy with daily sorrows, tears held back or shed, a total despair, scorching at times, then wan and empty."[2] In 1621, Robert Burton, describing depression as melancholy, wrote, "All my griefs to this are jolly, naught so damn'd as Melancholy."[3]

In my work as a pastor and as a pastoral counselor I have come to know many who have suffered from periods of depression. I have seen the effects depression has not only on the ability to experience the joys of life, the bliss of love, the depths of beauty, and passion for the true and the just, but also on the ability to make good decisions, or to make decisions at all. I have seen lives dwarfed, curtailed by depression because of options not taken, talents not developed, in the choice of life's partner or life's work. Then there is the secondary bitterness and resignation that such inaction and lethargy can breed. A terrible cycle of depression-inaction-bitterness-further depression can develop. Often these sufferers from depression conclude that they are flawed, that life offers little but crumbs, and that God is not worth the bother. It is heartbreaking not only to see the pain and emptiness of the inner experience of depression, but also to see its effects on the course of a life.

I have been both aggrieved and outraged at the high rates of depression and the low levels of effective intervention into this debilitating condition. Many depressed people do not seek help; the ones who do seek help encounter pastors, doctors, or even mental health professionals who do not always recognize depression. Even when depression is recognized by a professional, the intervention is too often ineffective. Therefore many people continue under the cloud of depression unnecessarily. A large part of the motivation for this book is to make pastors and pastoral counselors aware of both the features of depression and effective interventions. It is my deep hope that this book can contribute to the growing awareness of depression's blight and what disrupts its hold.

It is also my hope that this book will contribute to a growing body of pastoral care literature that addresses the needs of women. The dreadful condition of depression afflicts women at double the rate it does men.[4] If you ask pastors and counselors who comprises the bulk of the people who come to them for help, they will often answer, "depressed women." I hope to explore the question of why women are more prone to suffer from this slayer of faith, hope, and love—so central to the Christian life. What accounts for the discrepancy between men and women in rates of depression?

Multiple indicators suggest that what account for the differences in rates of depression is differences in access to power.[5] One researcher defined the power that depressed women lack as "the ability to provide for one's own needs and security and the needs and security of loved ones, to stand up for oneself in conflicts with others, and to make life decisions based on one's own desires."[6] The power discrepancy between men and women is well documented. Each year, between one quarter and one third of the women in the United States are beaten by a husband or boyfriend, and approximately 1,500 women and girls are killed by male partners. Until the 103d Congress (1993–1995) no more than 3 out of 100 U.S. Senators were women.[7] Today the Senate is 9 percent women, while women comprise 52 percent of the U.S. population.[8] Forty-six percent of women heads of households live in poverty.[9]

Not only is there a limited access to power according to these social indicators, but at a more insidious level there are far fewer cultural images of women as powerful. Women have tragically few cultural images of powerful women to draw upon in the creation of a self-image. Literature, movies, and television tend to depict women as less competent, less intelligent, and less assertive than men. Women are persistently portrayed as victims in popular media. Furthermore, the woman who is powerful, competent, assertive, and intelligent, and who refuses to be a victim, is considered less of a woman, less "feminine." Therefore the hindrance in access to power can be described in these two ways: the lack of social and political (or "external") power and the lack of "internal" power in the form of images of strong women. (I put internal and external in quotes because I don't believe we can split the self from social context, but they are useful explanatory terms.) The position of powerlessness increases the "external" life stress and decreases the "internal" protection from depression. Powerlessness brings more frequent and more intense stresses to psychologically less protected selves.

So this form of pain raises for the pastoral caregiver not only questions of the care and cure of the depressed but also questions of the just distribution of power, and how to appropriate the resources of Christian scripture and tradition. While depression for both men and women is the result of a complex set of biological, social, and psychological factors, power appears to be the one factor that accounts for gender differences in rates of depression. In seeking to address these power issues, I will be working from the assumption that the power that is healing for depressed women is not power as domination or coercion. Healing power is power as capacity, or skill, or effectiveness, a level of energy or creative efficacy or competence, the "power to" do or be something.[10] How to address issues of care, cure, and power in depressed women, and how to do so from a theological perspective, will be discussed in the following pages.

Since I am addressing the advanced pastoral caregiver, in chapter 1 I move immediately to a description of the particular model of depression that I assume, a model that takes into account interlocking biological, psychological, and social factors. Having taken this deeper look at depression, I then look at the theological challenges raised by depression. I make a proposal for a workable theological response, one that includes the views from the stance of the depressed person, the caregiver, and the scholar.

It is my hope that this book will be useful, providing to pastors, pastoral care specialists, and pastoral counselors not only an intriguing analysis of the problem of depressed women but also practical tools for the care of depressed women. Therefore, throughout the course of the book I will be suggesting pastoral counseling interventions. Because they will largely be informed by a cognitive model, chapter 2 gives a brief introduction to the basic principles and practice of cognitive therapy.

Speaking as a pastor and a pastoral counselor, when I attempted to come to terms with the pain of depression in women's lives, its connection to power dynamics, and the theological questions it raised, I found certain issues emerging again and again as critical in grasping the fullness of the phenomenon of depressed women. The first area, covered in chapter 3, is *social location.* The position of all women in a sexist culture, and the particular social location of an individual woman, are important areas to explore for an understanding of the disproportional numbers of depressed women. Depression cannot be understood as a result of isolated internal psychic processes. Rather, the place of a woman in the social sphere will profoundly influence her vulnerability to depression.

Chapter 4 addresses another area, the *self.* What happens to women's selves in a sexist culture? One of the effects of sexism has been called the "silencing of the self," or, as I have called it, an eclipsed self. Depression as an event of the self—and how the self is connected to the ambient social structures—are critical questions.

Chapter 5 covers an additional area of concern for women: interpersonal *relationships*. The impact of a woman's interpersonal connections is crucial to understanding her depression. Many feminist psychologists have noted that women tend to be particularly oriented to relationships. Sadly, some psychologists have suggested that this relationship orientation is a sign of an undeveloped ego, a manifestation of woman's excessive dependency needs, and responsible for the high rates of depression in women. However, feminists are saying that it is not relationship orientation that is the problem; rather, it is the nature of intimate relationship in a patriarchal culture that is the problem. In other words, it is the quality of these relationships that contributes to depression in women, not women's tendency to give them primacy.

Another core issue to explore is that of the *body*, discussed in chapter 6. Western cultures tend to view women as generally belonging to the bodily sphere as opposed to the rational or spiritual spheres. These cultures value women to the extent that they live up to standards of beauty, or for the reproductive capacities of their bodies, or for their ability to tend to the bodily needs of family and community. In addition, the physiological aspects of depression further implicate the body. Embodiment is therefore a critical issue to explore.

In chapter 7 the important issue of *anger* is considered. If you scratch the surface of depression, you will often find anger. This powerful emotion is often denied, repressed, feared, or reviled. Yet it is a sign of life, a sign of inner rebellion. It is a powerful resource for change in a woman's life. And it is often the response to feeling powerless. Some have understood depression as "anger turned inward," while I understand frustrated, inefficacious anger as conducive to depression.

Finally, in a discussion of depressed women, we as pastoral caregivers must give particular attention to the issue of *hope*, addressed in chapter 8. Depression is an illness that vitiates hoping capacities. As those who are grounded in faith in a merciful and powerful God, we give particular attention to the dynamics of hope with those who are depressed. Among helping professionals we are particularly qualified to address this central feature of depression: hopelessness.

Throughout this book I will continually be raising the theological questions of how scripture and tradition are part of the problem and how they are part of the redemption. I will explore ways to draw upon the rich resources in Christian narrative, symbol, ritual, and worship to address the issues of depression in women.

When I speak of "women," I recognize that I am almost always speaking of women similar to myself, whose particularities include being white, American, educated, middle class, heterosexual, Protestant, and of Northern European origin. Difference among women matters, and the material presented here is particular, limited by the selections and interpretations I have made to respond to the population of women I know best, those like myself. Therefore, this book, the clinical research it is based on, the psychotherapeutic theories and techniques espoused, the feminism advocated, and the examples offered, all bear the marks of my social location. The usefulness of this book may be limited to those in a similar place.

Julia Kristeva described her depression as "the loss of my being—and of Being itself." She said that "the depressed person is a radical, sullen atheist."[11] In this exploration of depressed women, women who often report not only losing their own being but losing divine Being itself, I hope to offer theories and practices that loose the sufferer from such an excruciating loss. It is for the sake of the women suffering from depression that I embark on the journey through the chapters that follow.

Chapter One

Women, Depression, and Theology

As caregivers, we know that depression is not unhappiness, grief, spiritual crisis, discouragement, the blues, existential alienation, or the deep dread of death. We know the difference between a widow's grief and depression, between being "down in the dumps" for a few days and depression. We know that it is a particular human experience with definable emotional, cognitive, physical, and behavioral manifestations. While we see many forms of human distress in our work as caregivers, we know that depression is a unique form of pain. In this book, when I refer to depression, I will not be referring to the many forms of distress of the inner world, but to what can be clinically diagnosed as major depression.

Yet we are not always clear about what gives rise to depression. What causes it in the first place? What makes some more prone to depression than others? Over the ages it has been attributed to everything from the position of the moon and stars to the body's "humors" and black bile. Today's thinking points to a confluence of biological, psychological, and social factors involved in the genesis of depression.

A Biopsychosocial Model

Current research strongly suggests that depression begins with the genes we are born with. As some clinicians say, if you want to avoid depression, choose your parents carefully. Most clinical researchers in the area of depression now believe that all people, men and women, fall somewhere on a continuum of biological vulnerability to depression that is genetically transmitted from one generation to another. At one end of the spectrum are those who are very vulnerable to depression: a small stress can trigger an episode of depression. At the other end are those who have a low biological susceptibility to depression. Great human tragedy can befall them, and they will suffer greatly, but they will not be depressed. The biological substrate is a very important factor in discussing vulnerability to depression.

So *biology* creates the scene. On this stage, there occurs the drama of human life with its joys and pains, delights and losses, loves and hates. The stresses of life can function as triggers to a period of depression, depending on how biologically vulnerable we are. Against this biological substrate the inevitable life stresses will have a greater or lesser effect on one's mood, depending on the inborn physiological vulnerability. Our bodies are physiologically more or less vulnerable to the stress triggers that life inevitably brings all of us. We live life as fully embodied, biological, physical beings, and the phenomenon of depression, which is so easily relegated to the realm of the psyche or the emotions and cut off from the body, illustrates this fact well.

Some have picked up on this biological basis for depression and suggested that the reason more women are depressed is that there is something inherent in female biology that makes women more prone to depression. Undoubtedly this is some version of the hypothesis of "raging female hormones." Yet a significant body of research shows that women are not physiologically "hard-wired" to be more depressed than men.[1] Our experience of menstrual cycles, menopause, pregnancy, and other physiologically female processes are not responsible for the predominance of depression in women.[2] It is women's social position of powerlessness that accounts for a significant difference in depression rates, not simply biological differences.

Even as we are biological beings, we are also shaped by our individual *psychology*. We inhabit an inner world with a particular landscape and psychological configuration. Though the nature of the inner world has been the object of speculation since ancient times, many of the caring practices of pastoral counselors and psychotherapists have been informed by the field of psychology, which has variously described the inner world. Whether we speak of id, ego, and superego, or good object and bad object, or automatic thoughts and interpretive schemata, we have some notions of the landscape and operations of the inner world.

One way to look at the inner world is that it is the site of meaning-making. We now know that human beings are fundamentally interpreters, and that no stress comes to us unmediated by an interpretive lens. The meaning assigned to a particular event will determine whether or not it is a stressor. For example, for the person whose psychological makeup renders them particularly fearful of being abandoned, a friend who does not show up at the appointed time may mean to them that they are on the verge of abandonment. For another person raised in a large family, the friend's tardiness may be interpreted as the joyful occasion of extra time for relaxation. These interpretive lenses are formed by our families, our significant life experiences, our cultures, and the communities in which we participate. An enduring insight into the psychological aspects of depression was contributed by Sigmund Freud: Whenever an event is interpreted as a major loss, then this functions as a particular powerful stressor. Any major loss, such as the loss of an important relationship or job or status or role, can be the trigger to a period of depression.

And finally, the *social setting* is an important factor to consider. More and more intellectual endeavors are recognizing the importance of the social and cultural context for understanding human problems, and this is an especially important factor in considering depressed women. Though depression is a tremendously isolating experience, and withdrawal from social interactions and the public world are key features, there are powerful social factors in depression's genesis. It is clear that those socially located to have access to various resources are less vulnerable to depression. For example, those with limited financial resources tend to be more vulnerable to depression, while those with access to support tend to be less vulnerable.[3] Therefore, both the incidence and the impact of stresses are always affected by the social structure.

This definition of depression, as having critical biological, psychological, and social aspects, can be understood in shorthand as a biopsychosocial model. All three aspects are crucial to a thorough understanding. This definition not only makes the assumptions of this author clear, but also helps the pastoral caregiver interpret it to the depressed person and her family.

An additional useful way of interpreting depression to those affected by it is to say that it is an illness. As the public health slogan says, "Depression is an illness, not a weakness." The definition of depression as illness makes several of my assumptions clear. First of all, illness nomenclature is helpful because it suggests that blame is inappropriate. Just as one would not blame a person for being diabetic, or suggest a person with high blood pressure should "snap out of it," or tell a person with leukemia to "get over it," or a person with cystic fibrosis to "shake it off," neither is it appropriate to give such responses to the depressed person. Blame is implied in such misunderstandings of depression as laziness or a lack of discipline. Some attribute depression to a lack of religious faith or an immature spiritual life. Others blame the victim by saying depression is a form of self-absorption, an excessive focus on one's internal feelings and moods. While many illnesses, such as some cases of heart disease and cancer, have strong connections to lifestyle choices, blaming the victim is inappropriate in all illnesses, including depression. Many have yet to realize that depression is an illness, a condition that affects a whole person, in all the pluriform manifestations that humanness implies. Pastoral caregivers can provide this important, useful interpretation of depression that removes blame from the sufferer.

A second assumption that the term "illness" implies is that something is wrong. Illness suggests pathology, something that is not health, something that should be healed. It is my assumption that depression is a departure from human wholeness. This is in contrast to those who speak of depression as useful or an important step on the way to health. Some refer to depression as a form of psychic cleansing, or a way of taking care of unfinished psychological business. It has been interpreted as a useful call to take stock of one's life and priorities, an important signal to make some life changes. Others use more spiritual language to suggest that it is a time of withdrawal or incubation before a period of spiritual rebirth, a psychic retreat in order to reconnect with the deepest self and with God. These interpretations of depression as useful are inconsistent with my view of depression as illness, a form of brokenness that calls for healing.

The third implication of the term "illness" is that depression is a bodily phenomenon. Illness suggests an event of the soma, a physical occurrence. It is the assumption of this book that depression is clearly a matter of human physiology, and the term illness strongly suggests that biological element.

These three implications of the term "illness" —the inappropriateness of blame, a departure from health, and a bodily event—all render it a very helpful way of understanding depression. It is an important interpretive tool for explaining depression to individual sufferers and their friends and families.

A word of caution to the caregiver is in order at this point. While illness is helpful nomenclature for depression for the reasons stated above, it must be remembered that the *mental* illness label has been used to control and silence women.[4] Under the label of insanity, women's legitimate protest against social conditions has been dismissed. The psychic deformations of patriarchy have been labeled individual mental illness without naming the contributing cultural power configuration. The purpose of the illness label is to lift blame from the individual woman, not to reinforce the stereotype of "woman as mentally inferior." Therefore the sensitive caregiver, while interpreting depression as illness, will be careful to avoid invoking such harmful stereotypes as the madwoman, the hysterical woman, or the chronically mentally unstable woman. The purpose of the illness label is precisely to avoid naming women's character weakness or psychic constitution as responsible for their depression.

A Lifespan Perspective

There is disagreement among clinicians about ways to classify depressions. Some suggest that depression should be classified according to whether it is biological or circumstantial. They make a distinction between a depression that is "caused" by fluctuations in internal brain chemistry, and one that is "caused" by a life event. Some speak of endogenous and exogenous depressions, or reactive and autonomous depression. They suggest that such categories as reactive and autonomous represent two decidedly different types of depression with different sources and requiring different interventions.

I advocate, on the other hand, a more integrated model. Rather than speaking of depression in terms of mutually exclusive dichotomies, either biological or circumstantial, this model takes a view of depression where the lines between categories cannot be strictly drawn. This model looks at depression from a lifespan view, examining the effect of stresses over a lifetime on those with varying biological vulnerabilities to depression. This longitudinal perspective allows the emergence of the breakdown of rigid boundaries between reactive and autonomous depression.

The lifespan perspective reveals some extremely important information for the caregiver. Researchers have found that 70 percent of those who have experienced a major depressive episode will experience another. In fact, it seems that the more episodes of depression one experiences, the more vulnerable one is to future episodes. Furthermore, it takes progressively less stress to trigger an episode of depression, the more episodes one has experienced. In other words, the first episode of depression requires more stress than the second, and the third episode is precipitated more easily than the second. The length of time between depressive episodes decreases as well. Eventually, after a certain number of episodes, the onset can become virtually autonomous, not dependent on an external stressor at all. So it becomes clear in the continuum model how the exclusivity between endogenous and exogenous, or reactive and autonomous, breaks down. At earlier stages of the illness, episodes are relatively responsive to stress, to external circumstances. In the later stages, autonomous patterns emerge, and the episodes become less responsive to external factors.[5]

An important topic of research has been to identify biochemical explanations of the clinical observations of the course of the illness. One hypothesis involves the notion of "kindling." It seems that if certain parts of the brain are stimulated regularly, for example, for one second a day, the first round of stimulations cause no response. However, as the regular stimulation continues, eventually that part of the brain does begin to respond. What is relevant to depression is that progressively greater physiological response is caused by identical stimulations. In other words, the level of the stimulation stays the same, but the brain increases its level of response to it. Eventually the brain's response becomes autonomous, producing the physiological response independent of the external stimulation. Using this understanding of the general phenomenon of kindling, we can see how repeated stressors, or repeated depressions, can have the effect of producing an autonomous affective illness.[6]

Experts Kenneth Goodwin and Kay Redfield Jamison have proposed that all depressions be considered either unipolar or bipolar. While the *Di-*

agnostic and Statistical Manual of Mental Disorders (Fourth Edition) distinguishes bipolar from unipolar depression only by the presence or absence of mania or hypomania, Goodwin and Jamison claim that there are additional differences in the course, onset, symptoms, and epidemiology of the two subcategories of illness. For example, patients with unipolar depression experience more anxiety and weight loss than bipolar patients, and tend to sleep less and have depressive episodes of longer duration.

Jamison and Goodwin's model is amenable to the biopsychosocial model. The various biological factors outlined above describe the genetically determined biological substrate of their model. In the context of a particular biological substrate, a person experiences psychological stress. The psychological stress can be of any sort that life presents, but is often in the form of a significant loss. However, stressors cannot be considered wholly individual events in an isolated person's world. Each of them bears some relation to human sociality. So social factors are also critical. The available environmental resources, the level of interpersonal satisfaction, and the level of economic security are all social elements that can function as stressors that precipitate depression. In sum, the biological forms the substrate, and the psychosocial provides the trigger.

Many clinicians and theorists who write about depression have yet to subscribe to the model of affective illness that Goodwin and Jamison describe. Many still refer to endogenous and reactive depressions as separate and distinct entities. In my opinion, this model best accommodates the biological, psychological, and social aspects of depression into a comprehensive, lifespan framework.

Theological Challenges

This account of depression will raise disturbing theological questions for the pastoral caregiver. When one considers the social power inequities involved in the higher rates of depression among women, one hears the trembling of the theological edifice most of us occupy. The phenomenon of women's depression shakes some of the fundamental pillars of Christian faith.

The most obvious theological challenge may also be one of the oldest that the faithful have faced: the question of theodicy. How can human suffering be compatible with affirmations of an all-loving, all-powerful God? Profound human pain should always rattle our theological bones to the marrow and leave us struggling to grasp the intellectual and moral implications of affirmations of God's love and power. Women's depression is no exception. It causes us to ask, How can the existence of such psychic pain, which disrupts relationships, creativity, and even the desire to live, be compatible with the compassionate, sovereign God we proclaim? To look into the eyes of a woman who is profoundly depressed, and to see that they are post-pleading eyes, eyes that once were desperate for relief from the pain, but that have acquired the pall of resignation to a living death, is to look into the core of the question of theodicy. How can this be, O Lord? Why is this happening in your good creation? If we are to raise the theodicy question at an empathic level, at an existential level, at a level of personal involvement, we will at once also taste the rebellion against such suffering in God's good creation. So the first theological challenge of women's depression is not a new one. It is the question of the incompatibility of the reality of human suffering with our faith claims of a loving and powerful God.

The second theological challenge poses the problem of an illness that hinders participation in central aspects of Christian life and faith. What does it mean that an illness cuts one off from the experience and life and comforts of faith? Depression hampers participation in Christian life and faith in at least three ways. First, hope is vitiated. Hope is a central mark of Christian faith, and depression virtually eliminates the capacity to hope. In fact, hopelessness is a key symptom of depression as described by clinicians. The ability to live in the hope of a loving, forgiving, liberating, justice-making God, the One who brought the Hebrew people across the Red Sea and whose resurrection power fills the earth, is the hallmark of Christian faith. To be incapable of this hope is to be incapable of participation in the fullness of Christian faith and life.

Second, depression hampers participation in Christian life and faith with its effects on relationships. The ability to give and receive love is greatly hindered. The blankness of feeling and the lack of motivation to act hinder both the emotions and the actions of love. Covenantal human relationship is fundamental to the Christian life, and such a life is meaningless to a depressed person.

Third, the suicidal impulse in depression is a fundamental challenge to affirmations of God's gift of life. Depression includes the impulse not only to withdraw from life, but also to extinguish one's life. Suicide is the most fundamental obstacle to participation in Christian life and faith because it involves the annihilation of life itself. What does it mean that a person can be prevented by disease from participation in such fundamental aspects of Christian life and faith as hope, human relationship, and the gift of life itself? This is a serious theological challenge.

The third challenge to Christian theology is to develop ways of thinking about community where, when the individual is hindered from full participation, the community participates on behalf of the sufferer. When the depressed person finds it impossible to believe, the community believes on her behalf. When the sufferer finds hope out of reach, the community hopes for her, and in her stead. When the sufferer cannot participate in relationship with the covenant community, the community nevertheless includes her, she continues to belong, she is a member of the covenant, whether or not she can feel it or act on it. By her baptism she is marked as God's own, and as a member of "a chosen race, a royal priesthood, . . . God's own people" (1 Peter 2:9). When the powers of darkness fill her soul to the point of suicide, the community will be there to stand by her, to watch over her, to never forsake her. A central Christian affirmation is that the sufferer from depression—in her isolation, her inner hell, her detachment from self, others, and God—nevertheless is claimed as God's own, and as a member of the body of Christ. This is an indelible fact.

The fourth theological challenge of women's depression is a feminist one, and it is twofold. First, at an overt level, we know that there are multiple places in scripture and tradition where women are excluded from ministry, they are told to keep silent in the church, considered unclean, not thought to be created in the image of God, called the devil's gateway, and so forth. It is not difficult to see how these parts of our past would contribute to the perceived and actual powerlessness of women, and therefore contribute to the problem of depressed women. By the grace of God, most mainline Protestant churches have roundly condemned this unfortunate aspect of the Christian heritage.

At a deeper level, the feminist challenge is more subtle and moves closer to a critique of core Christian claims. At this level, feminist theology challenges the Christian interpretation of virtue as self-sacrifice, sin as will-to-power, self-denial and self-renunciation as redemptive. Feminist theologians point out that such a glorification of powerlessness only vitiates attempts to redress power inequities and reinforces existing unjust power arrangements. The damaging, or at least problematic, effects of these traditional Christian claims is nowhere more visible than in the problem of depressed women. To lift up powerlessness as the highest form of good, and to frame the quest for power as the lowest form of evil, is to reinforce the internal and external powerlessness that gives rise to the high numbers of depressed women. Therefore, a feminist theological interpretation sees depression in women as a sign of patriarchal strains that are at the heart of Christian theology.

Yet the theological picture is still more complex. In spite of the overt and subtle problems with Christian scripture and tradition, feminist theologians point out the fact that Christian texts, symbols, hymns, narratives, and communities have, in places, functioned to support women throughout the centuries, and many women today report that they are sustained by their faith through times of depression. I have heard women say that it was only their faith that kept them going through their dark night of the soul. I have heard women say that, long after their own faith was obliterated by their depression, it was the steadfastness of their church community that sustained them. I have heard women say that clinging to a text of scripture, or a line from a hymn or sermon, or simply the memory of a pious grandparent was all the light there was. Christian beliefs and practices, it is clear, also function to sustain and uphold depressed women.

Therefore, the phenomenon of depressed women challenges us not only to take seriously a feminist critique, but also to find ways to understand what accounts for the different ways scripture and tradition function vis-à-vis depressed women. A thorough theological discussion will include the ambivalent role of Christian scripture and tradition.

Interdependent Theological Stances

In order to address these challenges raised by depression, the theological reflections will have to overcome dualisms that plague Christian theology: mind/body, individual/community, inner world/social power. Depression is clearly both a psychological and a biological event, a phenomenon that challenges mind-body dualisms. Depression is also a matter of individual-in-community. The norms and practices of community life must be addressed in order to understand and care for the individual depressed person. Depression also spans the traditional separation of inner world and external power structures. The private sphere of mood, the internal landscape, cannot be separated from the larger world and the question of who has access to concrete forms of power. Depression, experienced as a personal and psychic form of pain, has roots in the ways a social structure distributes power. All of these dualisms must be overcome if theology is to address a phenomenon as complex as depression.

Not only is the phenomenon of depression complex, but the relationship of theology to depression is also complex. What one can say theologically depends on one's stance vis-à-vis depression, whether one is a sufferer from depression, a caregiver for depressed people, or a scholar reflecting on depression. To speak theologically in the context of women's depression requires a clarity about the space one occupies. The theological perspectives of these three stances will take different emphases.

The first stance is that of the depressed person. What can the depressed person believe in the midst of depression? What is the theological world of the depressed person? How does she view God, God's relationship to her, and the ultimate horizon? To whom is she accountable? I believe her theological claims are accountable to her healing process, to her survival and restoration to the land of the living. What does she have to say to the tradition and what theological claims can be made?

Second, there is the stance of the caregiver. From this position theological claims have a double accountability: to the well-being of the depressed person and to scripture and tradition. Other literatures become relevant here: clinical studies, psychological theories, and descriptions of psychotherapeutic practices. Largely, the caregiver seeks to speak theologically in a way that subverts the grip of depression and restores a sense of self and connection to human community. Therefore, the fullness of the tradition is scanned for threads, themes, strands that function in a particular way: to heal broken psyches. The concerns here are pragmatic and transformational.

Third, there is the scholarly stance, accountable to scripture and tradition as well as the theological academy, in which the thinker reflects on the larger phenomenon of depression from a stance somewhat removed from the experience. This stance looks at the myriad intertwined aspects of the phenomenon, from the workings of the individual psyche to the power dynamics of social structures, and seeks a fitting theological response.

These three stances inform each other, acting much like a hermeneutical circle. Rather than a binary model that correlates disciplines, for example, an interpretation of the situation correlated with an interpretation of the tradition, this is a tripartite model that identifies three stances which mutually inform each other and without any one of which the understanding of the phenomenon is not complete.[7] The distinctions are clearly artificial. In one person may be present the intellectual rigor of the scholar, the compassion of the caregiver, and the insight of the sufferer. However, for the purpose of articulating the breadth of the various standpoints, a distinction is helpful.

The Stance
of the Sufferer

What is the theological world of the person suffering from depression? What can this person believe? And what is the significance of the experience of the sufferer to the caregiver and to the theologian? The following description of the theological world of a depressed person has been confirmed by friends, loved ones, clients, and students who have experienced depression. While it surely will not apply to all depressed people, it gives insight into a view that resonates with many.

The one suffering from depression often loses access to the things that give life meaning and purpose. In interpersonal relationships, there is a loss of connection to loved ones, the loss of the ability to feel their love. Any sense of past accomplishments or worthwhileness is lost, the past is construed as a series of failures or fleeting happy times that were just striving after wind, futile attempts at meaningfulness that really amount to nothing. The future is seen as a dismal series of unsatisfactory events adding up to uselessness. Creativity dies; play dies; capacities for the pleasures of beauty, food, touch, music—all die.

In this world "I don't care" and "It doesn't matter" become the mottos for life. Caring dies. Mattering dies. This is not the stripping away of the illusion of the importance of fame, approval, conformity, beauty, or worldly success, so that one comes to the core of what in fact does matter, for which one would give one's life. Rather, it is the judgment, not only that the illusorily important things do not matter, but that the core does not matter either. There is no core that matters. There may very well be a core, but it is not worth anything.

In this inner landscape God is not privileged when it comes to mattering. For many who are depressed, the meaningfulness of God dies along with the meaningfulness of everything else. God is not special when it comes to mattering. God may be far away and preoccupied. Or, if God is there, God is like an inert gas diffused into a closed room: undoubtedly everywhere, but utterly nonreactive, without effect on the sufferer, not affected by the sufferer.[8] God is basically irrelevant.

If anything matters at all to the depressed person, it is basic, rudimentary things. Getting some sleep, getting through another day, ending the inner pain, setting up the day so that the inner pulses of pain are minimized. The pain is often not relentless; it is more like a vacillation between inner blankness and inner horror. On a graph, the line would vacillate between zero and the nether reaches of the negative axis. What matters to the depressed person is surviving the next pain pulse.

For one who has lost the capacity to hope, when a configuration of biological, social, psychological, cultural, and political factors have rendered it impossible to hope, how can one speak of hope? Memory does not serve as a source of hope, because the past is interpreted in wholly gloomy terms. Nor does the present, which is bereft of hopeful signs, give any evidence that things will improve. Nor does the future, as there is no sight, no intuition, no sense that new life is possible. The only theological word for an existential stance that might be applicable is trust, a primitive, prerational trust. It is based less on reason than on desperation to end the pain. With this fundamental trust, the sufferer can seek psychotherapy and comply with the treatment strategy. With this trust the sufferer can choose to survive. This trust enables the sufferer to participate in ameliorative activities, such as sitting with loved ones, staying occupied with distractions, exercising. This rudimentary trust is hardly hope. It arises out of desperation, not glimpses of the possible.

So let us take what is central to a depressed person: sleep, pain relief, survival, outlasting the pain, a prerational trust, and any activity that is palliative and healing. It is in these terms that many sufferers may speak of God. This is the ultimate concern. For many persons suffering from depression, these concrete, vegetative, survival factors are the divine. Any palliative and healing factors can be considered of the divine. In the often tenuous fabric of the medication, psychotherapy, loved ones, pastor, scripture, exercising, videotapes, sermons, prayers, encouragement, empathy, determination, perseverance—all the caring and curing activities—God can be seen. Sometimes clinging to one factor, sometimes grasping at another, sustains the hour-to-hour, minute-to-minute struggle to survive. Any systematic theological statements must take into consideration this sense in which a depressed person might speak of God.

The Stance of the Caregiver

The stance of the caregiver must be twofold: the caregiver must occupy the world of the sufferer as well as the world of faith. The caregiver must empathically connect to the dark and hopeless realm of the sufferer and at the same time be compelled by faith and hope in a powerful and merciful God. The caregiver must know the world of the depressed as well as the world of hope.

The double stance of the caregiver gives rise to two sets of theological claims that become operative at different moments. In the *caring moment,* the caregiver will speak theologically with an eye to the effects of these claims. The theological statements are for the purpose of sustaining the sufferer. This judgment about which claims to speak to a depressed person will be based on an empathic understanding of the depressed person's world, as well as a clinical, psychological understanding of depression and what is therapeutic and/or comforting. The understanding of the God in the world of the depressed person will be taken very seriously, and a clinical understanding of the depressed person's hopelessness, helplessness, and negative construal of self, experience, and future will also be taken seriously. The caregiver's concerns are pragmatic and compassionate.

In this caring moment, the caregiver will speak differently to a severely depressed person and a moderately depressed person. For the severely depressed, the caregiving will be primarily palliative, offering a presence to the depressed person. The distortions of depression, as well as the manner in which one is sealed in the dank world of depression, render connections difficult if not impossible. A noncritical, nondemanding presence is helpful. The caregiver cares by gently encouraging compliance with the treatment regimen, not requiring conversation, finding a way to acknowledge the reality of the pain, to acknowledge that their depression is not imaginary, self-serving, contrived, or self-indulgent. It is also helpful to find a way to minimize the shame and stigma associated with mental illness by interpreting depression as illness, not moral or personality weakness. Finally, the caregiver can participate in the distraction activities: watch a movie together, play Scrabble, go for a run, talk about anything. The caregiver can provide the energy that the depressed person does not have by initiating activities and conversation, offering ideas for stimulating and nondemanding distractions.

For the moderately depressed person, caregivers can speak more directly of theological bases for hope. In so doing caregivers will not require belief, but simply offer what they believe as a way to support the tenuous strands of hope. The sufferer will be supported by those who hope on their behalf. The caregiver holds out another world, a world of hope as rendered in Christian scripture and practice, as an option that supports any dormant healthy beliefs that are struggling to emerge, take root, and gain ground. Speaking in terms of the cognitive model, theological claims of hope offer a response to dysfunctional automatic thoughts and support newer, healthier beliefs.

Having spoken of the set of theological claims operative in the caring moment, one can now speak of another set of theological claims that becomes operative in caregivers' *believing moment*. At this moment they will find within themselves the Christian beliefs that sustain and compel their speaking—theological claims about the love of God, the healing power of God, the solidarity of God with the suffering, the incarnation of God in Jesus Christ in and for the world, the quickening presence of the Holy Spirit, God's call to discipleship (which means the ordained ministry to some), hope in God who created bodies that heal and human reason that operates in the scientific endeavor toward healing ends, and so forth. All of these claims will sustain caregivers and enable the kind of compassionate perseverance required in working with the depressed person.

Yet in order to make the kinds of judgments about what is needed, selections from the tradition that are helpful to the sufferer, interpretations that are appropriate, and emphases that are therapeutic, the caregiver must also have in the believing moment a theological rationale for making these selections, judgments, interpretations, and emphases. The caring moment, in which there is editing and adapting of the tradition, requires in the believing moment a theological basis for such a treatment of tradition. Such a theological basis is a theology that makes truth claims with an eye to their effects.

The Stance
of the Scholar

The scholar is usually a step removed from both the world of the depressed person and the caregiver's "double occupancy," occupying both the world of the depressed and the world of faith. The scholar reflects on the phenomenon of depression as one who is not only accountable to the suffering person and to the insights of the caregiver, but also responsible for bringing scripture and tradition to bear on the phenomenon of depressed women in order to interpret it for the church. The scholar will be informed by the sufferers' experience of the meaninglessness of God, and the scholar will be instructed by the caregiver's insight that certain theological claims function to reinforce depression's grip, while others function to promote healing. The scholar is responsible for speaking to the church and the academy about how this experience and insight is brought to bear on interpretations of the word of God for today.

So how does the scholar interpret women's depression? There are four levels of interpretation. First, at the individual level, depression is a form of human suffering that calls for Christian compassion. Surely the church is called to give nurture and succor to those who suffer this distress. Furthermore, the church is compelled not only to offer care but to facilitate cure, to enable the healing process to proceed. We hear Jesus' voice, "Come to me, all you that are weary and are carrying heavy burdens, and I will give you rest" (Matt. 11:28). We recall the healing narratives in the Gospels. We remember Jesus who touched the paralytic, who healed blind Bartemaeus, who cast out demons. Depression in women is interpreted as human suffering to which God in Jesus Christ responds with compassion and healing.

Second, there is the corporate level. We know that depression involves not only individual suffering and brokenness but also social and political and economic brokenness. A discussion of the issue of power expands the response of the faithful Christian from simply calling for individual caring, to include a call for social justice. The descriptions of the bleak, excruciating experience of depression evoke sympathy and compel us to look for ever better ways to offer care. Yet when unequal access to power is named, the theological concern also becomes one of justice, not only of caring, and the need for a prophetic voice. We hear the voices of Amos, Micah, Isaiah, and Jeremiah calling for economic justice and advocacy for the poor and addressing the social structures that oppress and dehumanize the powerless. We interpret women's depression as one more cry of the oppressed to correct the structural inequities affecting women in contrast to men. Strains of liberation theology fill our hearts and minds.

Third, there is the level of critique of scripture and tradition. In addition to the liberationist perspective, we require a feminist perspective that not only lifts up liberationist themes in scripture and tradition but also offers a critique of scripture and tradition. We can understand depressed women as a part of the church's legacy of a sinfully sexist past and present.

Fourth and finally, there is the level of how our theological claims function. An adequate theological response will take into account that the same theological claim can function differently in different settings. The ways our truth claims function, both individually and historically, are critical theological considerations. We are compelled to be aware of the "effects of truth" in our theological claims.[9] We must explore what accounts for the different effects. Is it the quality of the interpersonal relationship? Will a truly compassionate and trustworthy person give a meaning to an utterance of scripture that is different from that of a scoundrel? Is it the economic system? Will a truth claim operate differently in the context of a community of the poor than it will among the affluent? Therefore depression in women can be interpreted to the church as an example of how our scripture and tradition can function in a variety of ways, that we must be attentive to those ways and be aware of the critical factors that enable our theological heritage to truly bear the gospel.

Depression is a highly complex phenomenon, it raises complicated theological questions, and it requires a broad, complex theological response. The stances of the sufferer, the caregiver, and the scholar are all required if one is to have the breadth of vision necessary to understand depression theologically. No one stance is adequate; all three together will enable the theologian to respond empathically, usefully, and faithfully.

Chapter Two

Cognitive Therapy

One of the most difficult experiences for pastoral caregivers is feeling help-less in our attempts to help. To be with someone in pain and to feel unable to offer comfort, advice, wise therapeutic intervention, or encouraging spiritual succor is very difficult for those who are called to care. Even some-thing as basic as our presence, our solidarity, often cannot be received by one who is severely depressed. The pain of the "helpless helper" does not necessarily arise from a naive desire to "fix things" or a narcissistic desire to be successful or feel personally powerful. The pain can arise from coming face to face with our own limits and from confronting intractable human suffering.

Depression can be one of those forms of intractable suffering, but most often it is not. The two most hopeful statements one can make about de-pression are, first, that in many cases it will eventually lift on its own. If al-lowed to take its course, the cloud of depression will usually pass. Depression is often episodic, and many find that individual episodes do end of their own accord. Yet it is a costly decision to allow depression to run its course. In the short term, it involves great emotional suffering. In the long term, it in-creases the likelihood that another episode will ensue. Therefore, the sec-ond hopeful statement is far more positive: depression is very responsive to treatment. Most sufferers from depression can be significantly helped by a combination of medication and psychotherapy. Approximately 80 percent of people who receive quality care experience relief. The news on the treat-ment of depression is very, very good. We as caregivers can be reassured, and we can reassure those for whom we care, that to be depressed is not nec-essarily to be consigned to a lifetime of "soul pain." There are effective in-terventions for depression, and we can all be grateful.

One of the most effective forms of psychotherapy for depression is cog-nitive therapy.[1] This form of therapy is offering pastoral theology a new conversation partner in the field of psychology. Though this book takes a cognitive therapy approach to the understanding of depression among women, I will briefly review the important contribution that psychoanalytic thinking has made.

The Psychoanalytic Contribution

Psychoanalytic accounts point to the interlocking phenomena of loss and anger in depression. When a person loses a significant object, there is a mixture of love for the lost person and anger over abandonment. The energy of this ambivalence is then turned toward oneself in an attempt to hold on to the lost one. In psychoanalytic language, the libidinal energy that was directed outwardly to the object becomes transferred to the ego in an attempt to incorporate the lost object into the self. Depression is the result of this anger turned toward the ego.

Freud wrote an illuminating piece comparing "melancholia" to "mourning." The comparison of depression to grieving shows some of the similarities in both the genesis and the symptoms of each, as well as highlighting the marked differences. Both originate in a loss of some sort, whether it is the loss of a person or a life situation. According to Freud, "the exciting causes due to environmental influences are, so far as we can discern them at all, the same for both conditions."[2] After describing the features of melancholia, Freud claims, "The disturbance of self-regard is absent in mourning; but otherwise the features are the same."[3]

The melancholic displays something else which is lacking in mourning—an extraordinary diminution in self-regard, an impoverishment of ego on a grand scale. In mourning it is the world which has become poor and empty, in melancholia it is the ego itself.[4] In this description of the distinctiveness of melancholia, Freud gives a poignant rendering of the particular pain that is depression. It is the injury to the ego that is manifest in an "extraordinary diminution in his self-regard" that distinguishes melancholia from mourning.

Yet psychoanalysis omits critical aspects of an adequate theory and treatment of depression of women. First, in the attention to the intrapsychic, the impact of the cultural context is minimized. Though Freud was certainly aware of society's contribution to personal unhappiness,[5] this attention to the depressogenic effects of a disempowering cultural context is not included in the practice of classical psychoanalysis. Second, psychoanalysis has not given adequate attention to the importance of power dynamics in the interpersonal realm. Psychoanalyst Marie McGuire describes this failure as the "refusal to acknowledge the psychic consequences of male power."[6] Feminists within the field are recognizing the importance of gendered power differences and incorporating this into their theory and practice.

Most skillful psychotherapists, regardless of their preferred theoretical approach to depression, including those with a psychoanalytic orientation, take an eclectic approach to the treatment of their clients. One of the ways a strictly psychoanalytic approach has been used to the detriment of depressed people is in failing to provide some of the directive interventions required to relieve the pain of depression. Because one of the features of depression is a lack of energy, motivation, and concentration, the therapist must be an active participant in the conversation, making concrete suggestions about steps that can relieve the immediate painful symptoms of depression. This has not always been recognized by those taking an exclusively psychoanalytic approach.

In spite of these shortcomings, psychoanalysis has made enduring positive contributions to the treatment of depression. It has correctly identified the central role of loss in the etiology of depression and has theorized the presence of anger and how it relates to the loss. The careful attention to the therapist-client relationship is another lasting contribution, though the particulars of the relationship vary. Finally, the understanding of the injury in depression occurring in the ego itself captures the depth of pain and the sweeping debility involved in depression. This locating depression at the very core of what constitutes a self is consonant with the experience of many who have been depressed.

More and more, however, pastoral theology is turning toward what have been called "brief therapies" as primary partners in dialogue.[7] For parish pastors brief therapies are amenable to the short-term counseling that is most common in the congregational setting. Many therapists and pastoral counselors report the effectiveness of cognitive therapy. Because this is such an important skill for pastoral caregivers to have at their disposal, I will devote this chapter to an exploration of its main features.

An Introduction
to Cognitive Therapy

Cognitive therapy was developed by Aaron Beck as part of what has been called the "cognitive revolution" in the 1960s.[8] This form of therapy recognizes the close relationship between thought and feeling. What a person is thinking will affect her emotions. The cognitive assessment of a situation has a great deal to do with the affective response, the mood it engenders.

Rather than speaking of the inner world in terms of id, ego, and superego, the cognitive model envisions the inner world as composed of interpretive lenses. There are basic interpretive *schemes* about such central themes as the self, the nature of the world, how others behave, an assessment of the past, the good, and so forth. These schemes are largely formed from childhood experiences of family, culture, religion, and the like. These basic schemes organize various *beliefs* about the meaning of experiences as wide-ranging as other people, bodily sensations, emotional arousal, memories, and philosophies of life.

The beliefs give rise to interpretations that take the form of specific cognitions called *automatic thoughts.* These subtle yet powerful thoughts exert a strong influence on affect. Automatic thoughts are preconscious, just under the surface of awareness, though available to one who has learned to become aware of them. They seem to appear involuntarily, spontaneously. Because they are prereflective, and not immediately conscious, they are usually accepted as a true and reliable assessment of the situation. For that reason, they are powerful shapers of mood.

The inner world, then, could be said to be organized in this way, from deeper, more static levels to more surface and malleable levels: interpretive schemes, beliefs, automatic thoughts. Relatively permanent schemes give rise to certain beliefs that shape our reading the world. The specific content of the reading is in the form of automatic thoughts, which are closely associated with affect.

A person who is not depressed will have a realistic reading of the world based on healthy interpretive schemes and beliefs. This person, however, upon becoming depressed, will read the world through distorted, negative lenses. Depression can be understood as associated with the activation of dormant, depressogenic schemes that give rise to negative thoughts. Stresses, such as a major loss, can call forth previously inactive, negative schemes for interpreting the world, self, and others. The person who is vulnerable to depression will have negative, distorting deep schemes and beliefs that, while often dormant, are activated by stress and accompany depression.

Central to the cognitive model's understanding of depression is the notion of the cognitive triad: a negative view of self, experience, and the future. The self is judged as inadequate and defective, unworthy and incompetent. Experiences are construed as defeat and failure. The future appears to hold only further unhappiness, hardship, and frustration. The cognitive triad is the cornerstone of the cognitive model's understanding of depression.[9] An example would be helpful. Clara is a person with a deep schema that says she is unlovable. She interprets the world through the lens that tells her: "I am only lovable if I am perfect." Therefore when she spills her coffee at a dinner party with friends, she has the automatic thought, "They will refuse my friendship." This thought, which she believes without question, gives rise to depressed affect. In some ways there is a logic to the relationship between Clara's automatic thought and her affect: anyone who was convinced that she was on the verge of losing all her friends might experience a depressed mood. Clara's perception of the situation was, in fact, not accurate. Clara's thoughts were clearly distorted versions of the truth; her friends still cared very much for her and rendered no negative judgment on her coffee spill.

Clara's "cognitive distortions," the automatic thoughts associated with depression, are characterized by distortions in logic. They can be categorized according to type of distortion, distinguished by the pattern or style of warping perceptions. Some of the distortions are as follows: *All-or-nothing* thinking. This results in seeing the world in either/or categories: "Either I am good or I am bad." "If I make one mistake I am thoroughly incompetent." "Everyone must like me or I am not at all desirable." Some cognitive therapists believe that this distortion is at the base of all the rest. The other distorted patterns of thinking could be summarized in this one. Another distortion is *overgeneralization*. One event, characteristic, or error is seen as definitive of the whole: "Because I am often late, I am a disgusting human being." Another distortion is *selective abstraction*, in which one feature is emphasized and others are ignored. The one C+ grade is the object of excessive emphasis at the expense of the five A+ grades, for example.[10]

The insidious nature of cognitive distortions is that they subvert any evidence that might disprove the underlying beliefs and schemata that make one prone to depression. These schemata are therefore self-perpetuating. Any experiences, feedback, or perceptions that may call into question the veracity of the dysfunctional assumptions and beliefs are selectively ignored, distorted, or discounted. Cognitive distortions provide the mechanism for perpetuating the dysfunctional thoughts.

Psychotherapy, then, involves changing the dysfunctional interpretive schemes, distorting beliefs, faulty cognitive processing, and automatic thoughts that give rise to a depressed mood. Therapist and client together treat dysfunctional beliefs and thoughts as hypotheses to be tested. The therapist collaborates with the client in devising means of assessing the validity of these beliefs. For example, Clara's therapist might ask if Clara is willing to treat as a testable hypothesis the notion that her friends will reject her if she is not perfect. From there the therapist can lead Clara through a process of Socratic questions and answers. "Do you have any friends now? Have you ever made a mistake? Can you think of a specific time when you made a mistake, even a big one? Did all your friends desert you at that time?" These questions lead Clara through a process of "guided discovery" in which she slowly begins to question the validity of her dysfunctional beliefs.

Cognitive therapy also makes use of "homework" to test dysfunctional beliefs. When a depressed mood descends, clients are encouraged to note the bare facts of the situation, along with the automatic thoughts. Next the client looks for distortions in the automatic thoughts and is encouraged to come up with a challenge to the automatic thoughts based on a more accurate assessment. The client then considers the following questions: (1)

What is the evidence for this automatic thought? Does your conclusion follow from the evidence? (2) Is there an alternative explanation? Can you see this from another perspective? (3) What is the worst that could happen? Could you live through it? What is the best that could happen? What is the most realistic outcome? (4) What is the effect of this thinking? (5) What should you do? What can you do about it?[11] By quickly considering this list of questions, the client often sees the distortions of the automatic thought come to light, and the client is able to make a more realistic, and less depressogenic, assessment. This homework often provides some degree of immediate relief to painful affect as well as challenging more deeply seated belief systems.

Cognitive therapy also makes use of behavioral interventions. Clara may be assigned to commit a social faux pas intentionally to see if, in fact, her friends will abandon her because of her imperfection. This would be considered a behavioral experiment to challenge a cognitive distortion. Another technique is to counsel acting "as if." The client with doubts about her social desirability may be counseled to act "as if" she were an interesting and attractive person, even if her doubts linger inside. "Trying on" new behaviors that are consonant with new beliefs, even if the client is not convinced of the veracity of these beliefs, can surface experiential evidence for their validity.

The question often arises at this point in a description of cognitive therapy: what if the automatic thought is an accurate one, and not a distortion of reality? Another related question is, Aren't there truly depressing things in the world? Yes, there are profoundly disturbing and grief-producing and discouraging things in the world that fill us with despair and angst. Yes, it is true that, in our lifetimes, there will almost certainly continue to be racism, sexism, and classism, and many of us will be victimized by it, and some of us badly. Yet the painful awareness of this fact, not only in a general sense but in daily, particular incidents, is not the same as the pain of depression. Depression is a result of distorted thinking, not of a realistic assessment of the human condition.

In fact, a falsely optimistic view of the world might be depressogenic. For example, "All hardship is only in the mind of the sufferer, therefore only weak and undisciplined people suffer." This belief might give rise to vulnerability to depression whenever hardship is experienced because it is attributed to individual failure. Therefore, cognitive therapy does not counsel positive thinking, or a rosy view of self and world. Rather it is concerned with an accurate assessment of things.

Another depressogenic distortion of "reality" might be, "Because I am a woman in a patriarchal world I will never know mutuality in relationship, I will never know vocational fulfillment, and my voice will always be silenced, and my body and soul will be forever hideously deformed by the ravages of patriarchy." It is not difficult to detect the globalization, the all-or-nothing thinking, the rigidity of categories in this line of thought. Yes, being a woman involves suffering the damage done by patriarchy, and no woman can escape it, but most of us would agree that this fact does not negate the presence of love, the beauty of nature, the power of sisterhood, the islands of sanity and mutuality, and the possibility for living and thriving here and there, from time to time, in God's good creation. The belief that women are utterly obliterated by patriarchy is a distortion of the possibilities for women's lives, even under the evil of patriarchal oppression. Depression is, by definition, based on a distorted view of things, and it denies all these possibilities.

Cognitive Therapy in the Parish Setting

Cognitive therapy offers a variety of cognitive and behavioral techniques that the pastor can appropriate. At the coffee hour, chatting with Ellen as she proclaims that there are no available jobs left on the East Coast, the pastor can ask simply, "Is that really true?" Or sitting at the hospital bedside of the avid tennis player who has just had a heart attack and is grieving the loss of a favorite sport, one can find ways to ask if there are truly no other enjoyable sports out there, if a year-long hiatus from tennis will truly destroy one's serve, and so forth. While this is far from "look at the bright side of life" thinking, it is a way to gently offer a more accurate assessment to those we are caring for.

Many of us have been taught that empathic presence is the only healing mode in the pastoral role. "It must be very sad to think of not playing tennis." "I can see that tennis means a lot to you and that you will miss the friends you saw regularly." "I sense some anger with God over your heart condition." While empathy plays an extremely important role, that stance alone can fail to empower another and allow debilitating distortions to continue, leaving a person alone groping for hopeful signs. It is appropriate to speak of sadness, but it is also appropriate to be aware that a person is laboring under the distortion that a favorite sport is gone forever, that particular set of friends is accessible exclusively at the tennis club, and that there is only one sport in the world that will ever be satisfying to her. In other words, gently correcting the distortion is part of the healing process.

While engaging in this "questioning," however, the pastor must always be aware of the position of power that she or he occupies. With women especially, calling into question cognitive distortions must not take the form of the "expert" pastor calling into question her "muddled thinking." Women's ability to reason adequately is already questioned by sexist cultural assumptions. Our "questioning" must rather take the form of speculating about alternative ways of looking at things, not corrections of "bad thinking."

A Typical Course of Therapy

First, cognitive therapy emphasizes the importance of the qualities of any good therapeutic relationship, such as accurate empathy, warmth, and a strong therapeutic alliance. Beginning to establish this kind of relationship is important, but the focus of the first session is to provide some relief from the troubling symptoms of depression. At this earliest stage the therapeutic interventions tend to be more behavioral than cognitive. The difficulty in concentrating associated with depression, as well as the tendency to withdraw socially, sleep a lot, and succumb to low energy levels, tends to make specifically behavioral interventions more effective at this early stage.

The therapist and client, or pastor and parishioner, begin by choosing "target symptoms" to treat, and together they choose exercises for addressing them. Since depression is manifest in affective, motivational, cognitive, behavioral, and physiological symptoms, Aaron Beck proposes techniques for dealing with each one of them. For example, he describes a "diversion" exercise to relieve acute affective pain. The client focuses on visual images, sensory awareness, conversation, and other forms of external stimulation in order to take the edge off the inner pain.[12] To counter the problem of low motivation to accomplish certain tasks, he recommends attempting the avoided tasks on a short-term basis.

It is of critical importance at this early stage that the therapist or pastoral counselor be active, providing the energy, hope, or thought that is denied the depressed client. When the client is very depressed, the therapist is more directive than at later stages of therapy. One very helpful behavioral technique is to schedule the upcoming week's activities. The therapist and client, or pastor and parishioner, together plan the week to include activities that give a sense of "mastery" and "pleasure." Activities in which the parishioner feels competent and activities that give the client pleasure are effective in improving mood. The parishioner can also be encouraged to keep a record of the week and to note the level of mastery and pleasure in the various activities. This gives the pastor a picture of a parishioner's activity level, as well as giving the parishioner insight into the correlation between improved mood and activities that give a sense of mastery and pleasure.

The second stage comes after some relief from painful symptoms. Now the therapist and client include more cognitive interventions. This involves teaching a client to recognize and record automatic thoughts and give healthy responses. The therapist can teach a client how to keep a "thought record," where depressogenic thoughts, and their healthy rejoinders, are recorded.[13] The pastoral counselor may guide the client as she fills out a thought record in the session. The therapist will initially give examples of healthy responses, then coach the client to find them. Eventually the client takes the thought records home and fills them out when experiencing a depressed mood. Although the therapist may have been quite directive during the earlier stage of depression, at this point the relationship becomes more egalitarian.

Finally, the therapy moves to challenge the deeper, organizing depressogenic beliefs and schemes that are not immediately consciously available. These beliefs begin to emerge in the therapeutic process as consistent themes or rules that underlie negative ideation. The therapist and client work as a team to identify and test the accuracy and usefulness of these assumptions. One method was discussed earlier—naming the situations that support the old dysfunctional belief and vigilantly seeking situations that support the newer, healthier belief. Another method is asking the client to list the advantages and disadvantages of maintaining an old belief. Usually it becomes clear that, while there may be understandable reasons for holding on to a dysfunctional belief, the old belief is nevertheless costly. As the therapy progresses, the client assumes more responsibility for both identifying and testing these assumptions. The therapist takes a supportive and suggestive role. Therapy concludes with an exploration of lifelong avenues of growth and development.

Cognitive Therapy and Women

Because cognitive therapy deals with the realm of belief and basic assumptions about fundamental aspects of human life, it is amenable to pastoral counseling. After all, as theologians and pastors not only are we comfortable with the realm of belief and truth, but we are accountable to particular beliefs and truth claims. If pastoral counseling is to be unique among the helping professions as having a particular relationship to a set of beliefs, then cognitive therapy offers one helpful approach. Of course the debates will continue about the role of "proclamation" in pastoral counseling, and certainly good pastoral counseling does not rigidly impose orthodox belief. But we still must struggle with the truth claims we live by, and how they inform the care and counsel we give.

Cognitive therapy can make a significant contribution to the pastoral care of depressed women. In addition to being clinically effective, it offers a way to connect the external culture with the internal state of depression. In a simplified fashion, one can say that women are depressed because the culture supports "depressogenic" assumptions, schemes, and behavioral patterns. For example, the cognitive triad (i.e., negative thoughts about the self, experience, and the future) meshes well with negative cultural views of women. Women learn from the dominant culture that their opinions, work, ideas, accomplishments—in short, their *selves*—are not as valued as those of men. Women learn to evaluate their *experiences* as unimportant, derivative of others' experiences, and having a lower estimation of success.

Women tend to believe the *future* offers fewer opportunities; expectations are lower, the possibility of reaching goals more remote. These are certainly generalizations, but they summarize some cultural attitudes that are harmful to women's mental health. Aaron Beck and Ruth Greenberg state:

> It is hard to dispute the contention that our culture tends to view women as ineffectual, dependent, and overly emotional, and troubled or depressed women as pathetic or manipulative. No doubt the fact that the culture confirms her negative self-evaluations is an added obstacle to the woman who becomes depressed.[14]

Cognitive therapy, like all psychotherapies, can be misused in the care of women. Such a misuse would be claiming that the problem of depression in women lies only in a woman's perceptions. In other words, the problem lies in the individual woman's depressogenic cognitive set, and not in the surrounding culture. Accordingly, all that has to be done is to change the individual woman's interpretive schemes and assumptions, and all will be well. This approach ignores the impact of the social and cultural factors we have discussed.

In fact, many of women's negative assessments of the future, the world's openness to women's voices, and so forth, are completely accurate, and not a matter of twisted perception. That we live in a world that takes women less seriously than men is not a distortion. Women don't just think they are undervalued and that there are limited possibilities; it happens to be true. Therefore it is important not to claim that "women see themselves as shackled long after the shackles have been removed."[15] A misuse of cognitive therapy is to discount a woman's account of patriarchy's effects on her life, and to fail to see the impact of cultural beliefs and power arrangements.

Some in the field of cognitive therapy are ensuring that this misuse does not continue. Denise Davis and Christine Padesky describe a cognitive therapy that takes into account the surrounding patriarchal culture. They articulate some common negative beliefs that women learned from the surrounding culture about their bodies. "Physical appearance is more important than physical function." "Uniquely female body functions, such as menstruation, pregnancy, and lactation, are a source of embarrassment." "It is wrong to nurture and pleasure the self physically." "Physical appearance is the key to love, pleasure, and worth."[16] Each of these beliefs contribute to depression in women. They discuss various aspects of social living, including living alone, marriage and family relationships, and parenting. The combined beliefs that "I am nothing without relationships" and that "others always come first" lend themselves to women's depression.[17] Overcoming both these physical and these social depressogenic sets of beliefs that the surrounding culture fosters in women requires the adoption of a countercultural stance by both client and therapist, pastor and parishioner.

The risks and costs of this position must be named. They note the importance of "bringing society into therapy with women, [which] could mean changing some underlying attitudes and rules of our culture."[18]

Cognitive therapy provides a useful theory for those who want to establish the link between cultural attitudes and personal mental health. There is room for showing the crippling effects of sexism not only on such externals as employment, physical safety, economic independence, and the like, but also on the internal world of women's psyches. Furthermore, it makes it possible to demonstrate the importance of changing misogynistic, male-centered belief systems. These beliefs and images about women are not merely inconvenient, inaccurate, a nuisance, or an extra burden. In fact, they are highly debilitating, burdening large numbers of women with the pain that is depression.

Cognitive Therapy and the Biopsychosocial Model

Here is how cognitive therapy fits into this biopsychosocial model. *Biologically*, practitioners of cognitive therapy generally acknowledge the importance of biological aspects of depression and will recommend pharmacotherapy. In addition, it can be shown that thinking differently affects biology. For example, thinking fearful thoughts can arouse the sympathetic nervous system and cause anxiety, thinking erotic thoughts can cause sexual arousal, and thinking sad thoughts can cause tears to flow. It is clear that cognition and biology are closely linked. A cognitive intervention can affect the neurochemistry of depression.

Psychologically, cognitive therapy is an intervention at a subset of the psychological realm: the cognitive. How a life event, physical sensation, interpersonal interaction, or the like, is interpreted through a cognitive lens will determine whether it is a stressor. In other words, if the unsmiling face of a boss is interpreted as "fleeting and uncharacteristic grumpiness," this smilelessness would not function as a stressor. If it is interpreted as meaning that "my work is bad and I will soon be fired," then the boss's facial expression might act as a stressor. The cognitive model theorizes how some life events become stressors by virtue of the meaning they are given as they are interpreted through particular cognitive lenses.

Feminist psychologists describe a form of psychological stress, a depressogenic trigger, that women experience: the tendency to de-self or silence the self.[19] Cognitive therapy describes how the self-policing, self-negating, self-censoring, self-silencing interpretive scheme might be deconstructed. A scheme that takes the form of "be pleasing or you will never have a relationship," "you need a relationship for emotional survival," and so forth,

can be effectively challenged with cognitive therapy. These negative interpretive schemes that women learn from the culture are powerful reality-
creating, self-perpetuating, relationship-shaping filters that render women
depressed.

Socially, cognitive therapy recognizes the importance of interpersonal
relationship and includes interventions at an interpersonal level. Behavioral
homework in the interpersonal arena, such as the development of assertiveness skills and intimacy skills, are all part of cognitive therapy. A relationship with a warm, empathic, caring therapist is critical for the success
of cognitive therapy. Enlisting the support, cooperation, and education of
significant others is important in caring for a depressed person.

Therefore, cognitive therapy is a therapeutic practice that is quite consonant with the various elements of a biopsychosocial model of depression. Though the cognitive model does not theorize depression as
thoroughly as the biopsychosocial model does, nevertheless, as a form of
practice, cognitive therapy is an effective intervention into depression as
described by the biopsychosocial model of depression.

For the caregiver who would like to read further on the cognitive ther-
apy of depression, I recommend *Cognitive Therapy of Depression* by Aaron
Beck and colleagues (New York: Guilford, 1979) and *Feeling Good: The New
Mood Therapy,* by David Burns (New York: Signet, 1980).

Cognitive therapy is useful to the trained pastoral counselor because it
is so effective, and it is useful to the parish minister because some of the
simpler techniques can be quickly appropriated for the less-structured pastoral care setting. It is also particularly useful for intervening in women's
depression. Theoretically it is consonant with a feminist social/cultural
analysis of depression, and practically it is a form of therapy that can address the depressogenic forces that women experience in a patriarchal culture. The following chapters will make use of cognitive therapy as it relates
to issues critical for understanding women's depression.

Chapter Three

Social Location

We who are pastoral caregivers are accustomed to drawing on all our re-sources to respond to the pain that we hear from a person seeking help. We focus our minds, hearts, and spirits on the soul, unique before God, who has come to us. We listen carefully to the stories of pain and alienation, loss and rage, that unfold in the voice of the person sitting across from us. Of-ten it is simply the fact of making this person the recipient of all our atten-tion that is the most healing act. To attend fully to another is tremendously empowering. We know that to focus on another's life—her future, her pain, her anguish, dreams dormant, shameful corners, hidden sins, secret guilt— is often a highly redemptive experience.

For the care receiver, to know this gracious attending is to know the love of God for herself, just as she is, many times with ragged history and uncer-tain future, with the sense of having done everything wrong, having failed those one loved most. It is to know God's love for oneself, the one who may have fallen between the cracks of what is considered normal, successful, reg-ular, who is following no particular narrative, or at least not one nameable or recognizable to others. To experience the blessing of another tending to oneself with gentleness, care, and hope is a powerful experience of the grace of God. It is to know the umbrella of grace, the alpha and omega of grace, that encompasses all the ragged edges, the fragmented and contradictory story lines, all of the hurts, sins, and failures and shame that remain secret and sore, hidden and haunting. And it is to know hope, the blessed assur-ance that, ultimately, "all shall be well, and all shall be well, and all manner of thing shall be well."[1]

Attending to the utterly unique individual before us, in all the unrepeat-able constellation of details, qualities, and experiences that constitute the full-ness of who she is, may be the most redemptive, sacramental act we perform. Let us never lose the skill, the art, the charism, of this form of compassion.

Let us also remember, however, that part of attending to the precious, unique soul before us is recognizing that, for all her individuality, she is a profoundly social being. By "social" I refer to the interpersonal realm as well as the cultural and political realm. In other words, we are made and constantly remade by our fundamentally corporate, relational existence. The woman sitting in your office brings with her a complicated web of social affiliations and influences, and is the locus of political and cultural maneuvers. She is the site of multiple overlapping and contradictory and interacting social forces that are shaping her life events, her attitudes, emotions, the course of her life. Theologian Rebecca Chopp recognizes the profoundly social and political sources of depression. She urges us not to fail "to view the psychological violence today in major disorders such as depression without understanding the political ordering."[2] Should we as caregivers fail to do so, we "forc[e] the analysand to become adapted to a situation which itself is dangerously distorted."[3]

So, as caregivers we engage in a process of seeing and hearing that is focused both on the individual and the social. Our vision is at once close-up and wide-angle. Sometimes we are viewing something close-up, like the intricate thing that is a Georgia O'Keeffe flower blossom. Sometimes we are seeing a Dutch landscape in which we assume a stance from afar that situates the person in a social space. Both are required to fully attend to another.

This chapter takes the wide-angle view. I will look at the various depressogenic effects of a woman's social location. Primarily, I will look at the effects of being female in the United States in the late twentieth century. For to be female is to experience the inescapable effects of a social system that privileges men and disempowers women, a system we can call patriarchy.

Clearly there is no one way of "being female." Multiple differences of race, ethnicity, and class create different kinds of women, and women experience different patriarchies. Yet male privilege is one factor common to the varieties of women's social location.

There are two ways we can express the effects of patriarchy on women's psyches, rendering large numbers of women depressed. We can understand them as cultural beliefs and cultural power arrangements.

Two Means of Damage

The first means of damage is the concrete realities associated with the power discrepancies between men and women. This factor is a matter of differences in access to social goods, such as meaningful work, safety on the streets and in the home, political voice, and child-care assistance. Miriam Greenspan simply states that "oppression is depressing."[4] Though this is not an often-heard phrase, it makes sense that social inequity would have deleterious psychological effects such as depression. Again, Greenspan claims:

> As long as men as a group have power over women as a group, the power to institutionalize the ways in which women are defined, treated, and mistreated as persons, large numbers of women will be depressed.[5]

Victimization plays a large role in the social experience of many women. Approximately one-third of women have experienced childhood sexual abuse, one-fourth to one-half have been battered, and three-fourths have been sexually harassed in the workplace.[6] Psychologically, many of these women show the symptoms of learned helplessness as described by Martin Seligman: helplessness, hopelessness, low self-esteem, difficulty initiating change, and so forth. High rates of depression are found among groups of women who have experienced some form of victimization. A further complicating matter is the physical effects of such victimization that include head injuries, which may give rise to, or be confused with, depression.[7]

It appears that poverty is also correlated with depression, and at rates higher than the sum of the number of stressful events. In other words, even though poverty is associated with a greater number of stressful life events, the rates of depression among poor women are higher than the sum of the risk for depression for each event. In a large-scale study of depression conducted in five sites across the country, the relative risk of the lowest socioeconomic group was 1.79 when compared with the highest socioeconomic group.[8] Statistics regarding depression among African American women are sparse and conflicting, and the results are complicated by problems of misdiagnosis among many nonwhite groups, male and female. However, what is clear is that a lower socioeconomic status, measured by such factors as education, income, employment, is associated with higher rates of depression. In the words of one writer, "African American women are often overrepresented in lower socioeconomic groups and are, therefore, at increased risk to develop depressive symptoms and clinical depression."[9]

Women are expected to live up to an often impossible role as the only nurturer in the family, and as the primary caregiver, which also renders them vulnerable to depression. Women often respond to the needs of others at their own expense, both emotionally and in terms of time. Because women tend to be more tied into complex social networks involving spouse, children, elderly parents, neighborhood, and community activities, they have a broader "range of caring" than men, and this leaves them vulnerable to becoming emotionally spent.[10] The way our networks of care are arranged places extraordinary emotional demands on women. This is an important social factor contributing to depression in women.

The second means of damage is a matter of cultural attitudes and stereotypes, such as that women are soft, compliant, and giving—beliefs about women that are appropriated from the ambient culture. Greenspan makes the stark claim that *"femininity is depressing"* (emphasis hers).[11] This statement draws attention to all the subtle attitudes, behaviors, and emotions that are stereotypically feminine. Dependence, helplessness, passivity, accommodation, self-sacrifice—all of these qualities are considered feminine in our culture and all of them have been identified as conducive to depression. To relinquish a sense of agency and control, to mold one's feelings and opinions to those around you, to see one's worth as derivative of those you serve, all of these are part of this culture's definition of the feminine and all of them are clinically depressogenic. To be truly "feminine" is to be vulnerable to depression. Greenspan speaks of this as the double bind that women find themselves in: either one can be feminine and depressed, or one can be undepressed and considered unfeminine by the culture. What woman has not cringed at the thought of being accused of being unfeminine, domineering, shrill, masculine? Yet the alternative is to make oneself vulnerable to depression. The dominant culture fosters notions of femininity that do not contribute to women's mental well-being.

African American women, in addition to pressure to conform to images of femininity in the dominant white culture, "may internalize their role designation and the media's portrayal of African-American women into an unobtainable 'superwoman' or matriarch image."[12] The "unobtainability" results in feelings of failure and powerlessness, contributing to risk for depression. In addition to the lower socioeconomic status, African American women face pressures to conform to multiple and conflicting images.

In the media, women are consistently portrayed according to the madonna-prostitute polarity. Either a woman is an asexual virtuous nurturing mother, or she is an evil temptress bent on luring helpless men from paths of righteousness. Women, aggression, sex, and death, or women, passivity, and self-sacrifice are the two loci around which popular imagery revolves. The particular form this dualism takes for African American women is the mammy-seductress. The seductress image justified the particular evil faced during slavery: rape by white men who considered their female slaves ever-available sexual partners. The image of the dark, oversexed seductress was used to justify both these actions of white men and the resentment and cruelty of their white wives.

Being bombarded by these images from the media will inevitably affect the construction of women's psyches. Both of the options, the maternal and the temptress, contribute to women's depression: the passive "madonna" role with its self-denial is, as we will see below, conducive to depression; the construal of women who claim power and place in the public sphere as "prostitute" inhibits women from healthier self-images and behaviors.

Many aspects of being a woman in this culture coincide closely with depressogenic conditions for both men and women. For example, perceived helplessness has been associated with depression in both men and women. However, helplessness is more strongly associated with being a woman in the two ways mentioned above: cultural beliefs and social power arrangements. For women, helplessness is a distorted belief based on stereotypical notions of woman as weak and passive. While it is not true that women are in fact completely helpless, perceived helplessness is buttressed by the de facto differences in social power between men and women. Therefore, the culture will foster perceived helplessness in women in two ways: by distorting women's belief in their own agency and efficacy and by, in fact, limiting women's access to power. Because such depressogenic psychosocial factors as helplessness, both real and perceived, are more closely associated with women, more women are depressed than men. In addition to helplessness, there are other depressogenic psychosocial qualities that are associated with femininity and female existence, such as passivity, compliance, self-effacement, and dependence. It is the fact that these "feminine" qualities so closely coincide with depressogenic factors that accounts for the large numbers of depressed women.

Women and Access to Power

One of the elements that becomes clear in the above discussion of women's depression is that there are distinct differences between women's and men's access to such social goods as jobs, status, and financial independence, as well as differences in access to images of self as strong, good, and competent. One could speak of these differences as a disparity of access to power, not only "external" social and economic power but also "internal" psychological images of self as powerful. Yet, as I suggested earlier, the external and the internal cannot be separated. The mechanism for denying social power is not distinct from that denying imaginal power. The de facto power discrepancies and the images are part of a single apparatus called patriarchy. This system of power discrepancy takes different forms in different contexts, but is comprehensive in inflicting the internal/external damage.

I was among those observing a presentation by Ann Simonton on "Sex, Power, and the Media" that illustrated this relation between the internal and the external. The presentation very skillfully moved from pictures of women from women's magazines and other familiar sources, to less familiar advertisements in trade magazines or European or Japanese magazines. Finally it moved to images very unfamiliar to most women taken from pornography. What was most disturbing was that there was a clear continuity from everyday advertising's images of women to the overtly pornographic images. In both, women are presented as victims of male violence, with the assumption either that women like to be victimized, or that their beauty is connected to victimhood. For example, in the less overtly violent images, women appeared afraid, running away in a dark alley, anxiously looking over their shoulders at a stalker. In the more explicit picture, there were pictures of women screaming, or heads twisted as though just slapped. Eventually, in the pornography, we saw full-blown pictures of women being beaten and murdered. There was a clear continuity from a woman simply afraid to a woman beaten.

In another example, the continuum began with the fragmentation of women's bodies appearing in daily media as pictures of headless women wearing bras, two legs coming out of nowhere wearing pantyhose, or an enlargement of women's lips advertising lipstick. This fragmentation, as the continuum progressed to pornography, became grotesque mutilation on the cover of *Hustler* where there is a meat grinder, a woman's legs sticking out of the top, and ground meat coming out. In a similar manner, the advertisement of an expensive piece of jewelry, where the jewelry acts as handcuffs restraining a woman's hands behind the back of her nude body, flows into the pornographic images of bondage, whips, and chains.

All of this, and then we heard the devastating news that the public is exposed to 30,000 advertising messages per day.

I, and several of the women around me, spent a fair amount of the presentation with our heads bowed, unwilling to see these images. It was a profoundly disturbing presentation. Disturbing not simply because there is violent pornography out there, and out there in great abundance, but disturbing because the same pornographic themes and images are appearing more and more in newspapers that come to our homes, in magazines in the racks at the grocery store check-out line, on billboards, and in our living rooms for an average of six hours a day via television broadcasts, which are now almost one-third advertising.

The purpose of this presentation was to show the correlation between images of women and the incidence of violence against women. The message of these violent images to both women and men is that violence is somehow acceptable, or at least a part of our world that is here to stay.

If this presentation skillfully drew the parallels between *images* of women and *violence* against women's bodies, I believe one could also demonstrate the parallel between images of women in the media and violence against women's psyches in the form of rendering women depressed.

If I had the resources, I would collect images from the media that may not directly give rise to bodily violence against women, but that nevertheless do violence against women's psyches by bombarding them with depressogenic images of women. There are images of all women as dumb, stupid, incompetent. "Bad" women are depicted as fat, "foreign," dark skinned, older, angry, powerful. "Good" women are blond, emaciated, passive, compliant, agreeable, deriving satisfaction from clean clothes/house/toilet/carpet, and so forth. In fact, even if one looks away from popular culture and to the classic novels, art, philosophic renderings, and even scripture texts, one will be hard-pressed to find significant numbers of alternative images of women. While it is not likely that our historically amnesiac society would be inclined to look to these sources for alternative images, it is no comfort to know that they do not offer very many good alternatives anyway.

While the media presentation I saw certainly demonstrated violence against women's bodies, the images themselves were a form of violence against women's psyches. To portray woman as helpless victim, woman as dismembered body, woman as object of men's pleasure, has the psychologically damaging effect of normalizing violence against women's bodies. The prospect of violence in one's future, and the normalization of it, certainly contributes to depression in women. As you recall, a negative assessment of one's future is a depressogenic factor. For a woman, not only is violence a real possibility in the future, but she is subtly reminded of it, and its appropriateness, in the media.

I believe the presentation I saw calls for a theory that addresses the relationship between image and reality, between what is depicted in popular culture and what actually happens, between image and social structure, accepted behaviors, and psychological effects. One such theory is that of Michel Foucault, a French poststructuralist philosopher. His thought challenges us to see many aspects of human life implicated in the vicious web of violent images of women and violence against women's minds and bodies. Foucault describes a web that includes ideas, texts, notions of the truth, symbols, power structures, institutions, practices, psyches, and, most interesting, bodies. The presentation I saw is a vivid and disturbing illustration of a web of ideas about women, aggressive capitalist marketing practices, family practices that include wife abuse, passivity correlated with femininity, and what happens to battered women's bodies. I would like to show how such a web exists to render women depressed. My argument is not limited to media images of women and violence against women. This is only one example of how a web of ideas, institutions, and practices can function perniciously against women's bodies. It is my purpose to identify a similar and related web that functions perniciously against women's psyches. Foucault's notion of "discourse" helps us understand this web.

Discourse:
Uniting Internal and External

Discourse is Foucault's way of talking about the interconnectedness of language, institutions, power, subjects, practices, and bodies.[13] By language, modern philosophers generally mean words, ideas, concepts, symbols, gestures, rituals, stories, anything that signifies something else. In the above example, the pictorial images of women would be included under the category of language. The institutions implied in many of the images included marriage and family, government and law enforcement, marketing and advertising. The power dynamics were clear: the images reinforced a powerless position for women. Practices included battering wives and girlfriends, rape, humiliating sexual acts, and so forth. And the implication for women's bodies was painfully clear: women's bodies were photographed and used to sell a product, and in so doing, practices that do violence to women's bodies were justified.

I would like to suggest that there exists a misogynist web of institutions, practices, language, and psyches, which I will call "truth-of-woman" discourse, that fosters depression among women, a web that integrates the internal and external described above. Discourse, which is much more than ideas or concepts, is more a mechanism, apparatus, or strategy for the operations of power, and we can identify one that is characterized by certain damaging claims about the "truth" about women.

The truth-of-woman discourse includes notions of good women as passive, dependent, helpless, and self-sacrificing, bad women as strong, sexual, and independent, and women in general as incompetent and derivative of men. This discursive formation is played out in, and cuts across, power relations in the institutions of marriage and family, politics, church, education, finances, business—in virtually every realm of human life. It is this discursive formation that colonizes women's psyches and leaves them vulnerable to depression. The characteristics of women in this reigning discursive formation are the very factors conducive to depression: helplessness, feeling incompetent, passivity, self-sacrifice, and being undeserving of pleasure. The very qualities that protect women from depression, and that have to be called upon in the psychotherapy of depressed women, are the qualities of a "bad" woman, namely, the qualities of strength, independence, power.

In a discursive formation, this web of ideas, institutions, etc., only certain "truths" are possible. Foucault speaks of a "regime of truth." He defines such a regime as "the types of discourse which it accepts and makes function as true; the mechanisms and instances which enable one to distinguish true and false statements, the means by which each is sanctioned; the techniques and procedures accorded value in the acquisition of truth; the status of those who are charged with saying what counts as true."[14] In other words, truth is closely bound to power operations, a matter of power operating through "mechanisms" for telling true from false, or the power located in those who are authorized to declare what is true, such as those who get to be called "expert." Therefore truth is not an objective reality to be discovered, nor is it even a useful construct created by leaders to control us or to help us live better. Rather it is the result of power struggles, a matter of a regime, and it emerges as a result of the way power works. "'Truth' is linked in a circular relation with systems of power which it induces and which extend it."[15] What is true is what is in power.

Truth regimes function by excluding the possibility of even considering alternative possibilities of thinking, acting, choosing. Foucault asks the haunting question of the effects of these regimes: "But what is it impossible to think . . . ?"[16] Truth and power are bound up. The truth regime, discursive regime, I am calling truth-of-woman discourse is one that creates depressed women through an ensemble of ideas, practices, power, and psyches. This understanding of power does not name the bad guys. It refrains from saying that women are in the grips of a hegemonic, all-controlling power, something like Big Brother. Foucault refuses to locate the power in any one place. He resists naming the State, or a particular dominant class, or the bourgeoisie, or the corporation structure as imposing power from above. For the purposes of our discussion, he would refuse to name All Men as the problem. Foucault refrains from referring to a power pyramid, in which power is concentrated at the "top." Rather, he views power as fluid and unstable, something that circulates, not focused at the apex.

Foucault speaks of multiple diffused and local sites in which power operates in everyday life, power in the interstices. He speaks of "dispersed, heteromorphous, localized procedures of power."[17] He declares that such obvious power centers as the State "can only operate on the basis of other, already existing power relations . . . in relation to a whole series of power networks that invest the body, sexuality, the family, kinship, knowledge, technology and so forth."[18] For Foucault, it is at this diffuse level, localized in the most mundane of practices, that power exerts itself most effectively.

This analysis suggests that, for women, power operates in local arenas. One can say, for example, that the assumption that the mother necessarily has exclusive responsibility for the daily transportation to and from school is a localized operation of power. Another example of power operating locally is the daily, even hourly, internal battle over food and fatness, the punishing tyranny of images of thin women that emerges with every bite taken. There are the pernicious effects of sexual harassment in the workplace, that take place at the water fountain, during a meeting, in the minute details of interaction between male boss and female employee. Power operates at these local, dispersed, interstitial sites to render many women depressed. It is what happens to women's psyches at this local level that contributes to women's depression. The regime of truth-of-women discourse operates at this local arena to deform women's psyches.

Resistance Discourse

Where is the hope? Foucault is often criticized for creating a system that is closed to movements that might subvert dominant powers. Yet he speaks of engaging in a "battle 'for truth,' or at least 'around truth.'"[19] For Foucault, there is an ongoing struggle around "the ensemble of rules according to which the true and the false are separated and specific effects of power attached to the true."[20] Therefore, what patriarchy presents us as the truth-of-woman is really not a fixed truth. Rather, the truth about women is a matter of contest or battle. There is a battle under way about what is true of women.

Multiple conflicting discourses compete anonymously to create a location, or position, or what post-structuralists call a "subject position," for women. In fact, the individual woman is the site of many criss-crossing, contradictory, conflicting discourses. For example, the mainstream Protestant clergywoman may be the site of the conflicting discourses embodied in liberal Protestant theology, liberation theology, the woman's movement, capitalism, Doris Day movies from the fifties, and psychotherapy. Each of these discourses competes with the others to constitute a position for a woman to occupy, or to constitute a woman in the full complexity of who she is as a thinking, feeling, acting person. It is the existence of this contest that is hopeful. Static hegemony is not the last word, the struggle continues.

The hope lies in "resistance discourses" that would subvert, do "battle" with, the patriarchal truth-of-woman discourse. This resistance discourse, this web of ideas, institutions, practices, psyches, an apparatus much bigger than simply a concept or idea, that constitutes a "truth," operates in a variety of ways. This discourse might emerge in the concepts of feminist theory and feminist theology, or in the esthetic realm of visual arts and music. It might emerge in the strategies of women organizing for better health care, for safe streets, adequate housing, for access to safe and affordable abortions. It might emerge at the level of the interpersonal, in the painful renegotiation of household and child care duties within a family, or at an emotional level in a new found rage against sexual harassment or the joy of mutual friendship. Resistance discourses, and all the multivalence of the web that they imply, offer an alternative version of the vision and practice of what is true of woman. They are also present along with patriarchal truth-of-woman discourse, engaged in the struggle for truth. Thankfully, one can discern a resistance discourse that speaks of woman as powerful, competent, entitled to pleasure, that is embodied in alternative communities.

Foucault makes the radical, and radically hopeful, claim that "there are no relations of power without resistances."[21] In other words power inevitably begets resistance to it. And resistance is "formed right at the point where relations of power are exercised . . . in the same place as power. . . . [L]ike power, resistance is multiple."[22] Wherever there is the patriarchal truth-of-woman discourse, there is also, somewhere, a resistance to it. Even in the bleakest, most oppressive corners of male-dominated realities there is some form of resistance. Foucault suggests the power operating at a local, multiple, dispersed level is "accompanied by numerous phenomena of inertia, displacement and resistance."[23] He speaks of the struggle against domination as "located in the fine meshes of the web of power . . . where the concrete nature of power became visible."[24] This view of resistance contrasts with one that attacks hegemonic power "at the top," that does battle with the tyrant or the owners of the means of production, or attempts to topple the one at the top of the pyramid. Rather resistance takes place at the local level, "in the fine meshes of the web of power."

Perhaps the most dramatic way Foucault refers to resistance is in his phrase, "the insurrection of subjugated knowledges."[25] He speaks of subjugated knowledges in two senses. First, what has been "buried and disguised, . . . mask[ed]"[26] by all that would impose order and system on history. This is scholarly knowledge. He speaks of the need to "rediscover the ruptural effects of conflict and struggle" that have been left out of scholarly accounts of human history.[27] "Subjugated knowledges are thus those blocs of historical knowledge which were present but disguised" by scholarship that reinforced domination.[28] In this sense, subjugated knowledge is all the accounts of "rupture and struggle" which scholarly criticism can glean from the very historical accounts that sought to mask them. We can describe these subjugated knowledges as the stories of resistance to hegemonic power that have been written out of history as it is officially recorded— stories of women in scripture and church who have sustained the hearts and souls and institutions of Christendom for centuries by opposing oppressive practices, institutions, and ideas.

Second, subjugated knowledge is "a whole set of knowledges that have been disqualified as inadequate to their task or insufficiently elaborated: naive knowledges, located low down on the hierarchy, beneath the required level of cognition or scientificity."[29] Foucault gives examples of this kind of knowledge as "that of the psychiatric patient, of the ill person, of the nurse, of the doctor— parallel and marginal as they are to the knowledge of medicine—that of the delinquent, etc."[30] Rather than being a generalized common sense shared by all, it is rather "a particular, local, regional knowledge."[31] This knowledge "owes its force only the harshness with which it is opposed by everything surrounding it."[32] This is the knowledge that is rooted in the perspectives of those who are not consulted in descriptions of things, the knowledge in the form of folk wisdom, or models of survival in poverty, practices of resistance in the interstitial spaces of the welfare office, the bedroom, the workroom. These knowledges offer an alternative "truth" and make it "possible to think" outside the dominant discourse, thereby subverting it.

Subjugated knowledges are survival knowledges: the knowledge that led Harriet Tubman on her underground railroad; the knowledge that enabled concentration camp victims to make it from day to day; the knowledge that enables a single mother in poverty to maneuver the social services department; the knowledge that enables a woman struggling with depression to get out of bed and face another day. These are subjugated knowledges that offer resistance to dominant discourse.

Theology as Discourse

The question for Christian caregivers and theologians is, does Christianity function as hegemonic truth-of-woman discourse, or as resistance discourse? The answer is both. Christianity has functioned to reinforce, and even as a source of, patriarchal truths of women. Yet we also know that Christianity has had the effect of liberating women to full humanity.

Theologian Sharon Welch speaks of the "ambiguities of discourse that has both oppressive and liberating functions."[33] She looks at the mixed history of the effects of Christianity and critiques it for damaging effects, as well as affirming the liberating effects. She holds scripture and tradition accountable for their effects, and furthermore, says that these effects are crucial to an assessment of theological claims.

Welch uses the Foucaultian notion of the "effects of truth" to sharply critique the effects of traditional Christian truth claims. For example, she suggests the Christian discourse on sacrificial love can function to keep women in situations of violence and abuse. She quotes Mary Daly:

> The qualities that Christianity *idealizes*, especially for women, are also those of a victim: sacrificial love, passive acceptance of suffering, humility, meekness, etc. . . . Given the victimized situation of the female in sexist society, these "virtues" are hardly the qualities women should be encouraged to have.[34]

Welch adds, "The meaning of the sacrificial love of Jesus is not exhausted by its internal logic or its coherence with the historically available words of Jesus, but includes the social effect of the symbol in the lives of women."[35]

We can add depressed women's psyches to Welch's list of the oppressive effects of traditional Christian theology. Misogynist aspects of Christianity are borne out not only in keeping women in situations of abuse and violence, but also in depressed female psyches. Christian scripture and tradition have upheld practices that have fostered women's self-loathing, sense of helplessness, and self-silencing, in short, that are depressogenic for women.

Yet we know that Christian scripture and tradition have also sustained depressed women, have been sources of not only comfort but also resistance. Welch reminds us that the same truth claim can function in a variety of ways. After critiquing the notion of sacrificial love, she explains that it can also function to comfort the suffering as battered women identify with the sufferings of Jesus.[36] We could add that notions of sacrificial love have inspired courageous, expensive acts of resistance to evil and injustice.

Welch understands Christian theology not as an abstract set of ideas to be judged by their adherence to scripture and tradition, but by the forms of practice they create and uphold. The "effects of truth," the function of truth claims, become criteria for truth.[37] In the case of depressed women, theology has functioned ambiguously.

Therefore, we as caregivers and theologians are to be alert to the mixed blessing that is our tradition. We are to be conscious of the effects of our theological claims, because simple adherence to scripture and tradition is no guarantee that our use of theological categories will function in healing and liberating ways. For example, we as caregivers must be clear that the theological emphasis on helplessness of human beings before an all-powerful God that requires self-emptying and self-denying obedience is conducive to the self-silencing that is characteristic of depression in woman. A theology that overemphasizes self-renunciation is not helpful. We must take seriously the depressogenic effects of these claims. Welch's work calls us to attend to the effects, the function, of our uses of religious language. We are challenged to make theological claims in the hope that they will engender liberating, healing effects. For Welch, "authentic Christianity is that which liberates."[38] We can add, as carers for broken, depressed souls, that authentic Christianity is also that which heals depressed women.

For Welch, a way of approaching Christian scripture and tradition that is attentive to its effects is liberation theology. Liberation theology can be understood as a resistance discourse, one whose rationality no longer relies on universals and ontological foundations, but one that focuses on the historical and practical "effects of truth." She notes this rationality in liberation theologians Gustavo Gutiérrez, Jon Sobrino, and Dorothee Soelle. She quotes Soelle:

> From a Christian point of view, theory and praxis can only be seen in their unity, which means truth is not something we find or by which we are found, but something we make true. . . . The truth of Christ exists only as concrete realization. . . . Theological statements contain as much truth as they deliver practically in transforming reality.[39]

Welch sees in these thinkers "the practical concept of truth" or "a new criterion for truth: practice."[40]

We as caregivers and as pastoral theologians have the opportunity to contribute to this discussion of the "practical concept of truth." In our practice, in our work with depressed women, we have a unique vantage point. We see how theological truth claims function to shape women's mood and psychological well-being. We work on the "front line" and can see how overtly misogynist Christian discourse, and celebrations of the negation of the self, can render a woman more vulnerable to depression. We are in a position to make important contributions to the emergence of a feminist liberation theology that is conscious of the "effects of truth," the impact of the theological claims on women's psyches.

Cognitive therapy, discussed in the previous chapter, provides, in the terms of our discussion, a way to subvert the truth-of-woman discourse. Through cognitive therapy, a caregiver can begin to loose the bonds of oppressive discourse and begin to introduce healthier practices and truths about the self, the future, the world. In short, cognitive therapy has the potential to make it possible to think, and act, outside the dominant truth-of-woman discourse. Cognitive therapy can be a helpful strategy for resistance discourse in the struggle to constitute women.

Cognitive Therapy and Resistance

There are at least four ways that cognitive therapy's construal of the inner world as the site of interpretive schemes and automatic thoughts can be placed in the context of power and cultural practices.

First, *these cognitive structures, the content of the interpretive schemes and thoughts, are connected to the myriad discourses circulating in the world around us.* Cultural discourse provides the *source* of the thoughts and beliefs and assumptions. The specific content of an individual's interpretive lenses is rooted in discourse, whether it be the dominant discourse of American culture, or the discourse of a religious or ethnic subculture, or an ideologically based subculture, or the patriarchal truth-of-woman discourse, or any one of various subjugated knowledges, such as feminism or liberation theology. Furthermore, these discourses are intertwined with institutional and cultural practices and cannot be viewed apart from this larger context.

Second, *as caregivers, we must be aware of the power dynamics of various discourses, various thought schemes that produce the inner world.* It must be recognized that not all discourses are created equal, not all thoughts and beliefs are created equal. Some are associated with economic and political power, such as corporate business discourse or nationalist discourse. Others are associated with social stigma, such as gay and lesbian discourse. Identification with such countercultural discourse can be costly in terms of access to such goods as social acceptability, employment, and housing. Discourse is caught up in movements of power, and the individual client in psychotherapy functions in a world where power is exerted through discourse, where discourses are instruments to exert pressures, incentives, and manipulations. It is inevitable that our clients are situated in power relations, and it is critical for us to recognize it. The thoughts and interpretive schemes that are the stuff of therapy cannot be separated from the power dynamics of which they are a part.

Third, *the caregiver using cognitive therapy must recognize that the potency of dominant cultural discourse accounts for the persistence of some dysfunctional be-*

liefs and interpretive schemes. We know how difficult the change process is, and how entrenched dysfunctional beliefs and behaviors can be. For example, women's deeply embedded sense of low self-esteem and helplessness is reinforced by the dominant male-centered culture. We can interpret the difficulty of change in a Foucaultian sense, which would suggest discourse invested with great power does not easily relinquish its hold on women. Not only does the cultural context account for the source and persistence of dysfunctional beliefs and schemes, it also accounts for the sometimes costly, painful, and isolating effects of appropriating countercultural discourse in the therapeutic process. The cognitive therapist must be aware that some of the more healthy, yet countercultural, discourse that she is encouraging the client to appropriate as a new source of beliefs and interpretive schemes may invite retribution from the dominant culture.[41] Furthermore, the therapist must be able to offer strategies for helping the client deal with a culture that may punish a woman for seeking countercultural beliefs and lifestyles.[42]

Finally, *the discursive perspective encourages awareness of the caregivers' discursive locatedness as well.* Their judgments about what appear to be irrational or dysfunctional assumptions may in fact be rooted in a subculture with which they are unfamiliar or negatively biased. For example, the white, anglo pastor may face such lack of familiarity or bias with African American, Latina, or Asian parishioners.

Resistance and Psychotherapy

While the cognitive model articulates therapeutic change in terms of beliefs, schemes, and automatic thoughts, we can describe cognitive therapy in terms of competing discourses. A Foucaultian account of cognitive therapy would assume that in the therapeutic process a discursive battle is under way to constitute the individual. In the midst of this battle, the therapist may present a new discourse or evoke one dormant in the individual. Change can occur by combining or juxtaposing discourses in the therapeutic setting. For example, feminist spirituality can be combined with liberating, or juxtaposed with damaging, aspects of traditional Christianity to create potentially healthier interpretive schemes. Again, to say the therapist may "present new discourse" is not to keep therapy at a conceptual level. Cognitive therapy addresses the practices included in discourse. The behavioral interventions included in cognitive therapy can be seen as a practice of resistance at the "local level" where power operates.

Therapeutic change in the cognitive therapy of depression may include appropriating a more affirming discourse of the self, a more hopeful vision of the future, and a more empowering assessment of present experiences. In this discursive understanding of therapeutic change in cognitive therapy the therapist is construed as the trustworthy bearer of new discourse, evoker of silent latent discourse, and in such roles, supporting discursive change. This is a form of resistance at an interstitial level. Change is therefore the painful process of trying on new discourses in conversation with a trustworthy guide, sometimes failing, sometimes succeeding in resisting powerful and dysfunctional dominant discourse, risking exploring and being constituted by the new and unfamiliar.

A client's behavioral "homework" can be understood as interstitial resistance to institutional practices. The client appropriates new behaviors that are inconsistent with depressogenic ones rooted in depressogenic cultural norms of the acceptable. These new forms of behavior can be understood to be at the level of practice, and not just at a cognitive, discursive, or theoretical level.

The client is encouraged to participate in a new discursive community. A new "discursive community" is the language of discourse to describe what has been called "health maintenance." The purpose of health maintenance is the "discovery and development of a community of women who can work together to change power systems so that human growth and individual freedom need not be sacrificed to achieve the system's goals." It is a community that is "proactive, social, economic, political interdependence [*sic*]."[43] This discursive community is concerned with support for healthier beliefs, behaviors, and interpretive schemes as well as changing larger cultural discourse. In many ways, this can be understood as a form of the insurrection of subjugated knowledges that Foucault describes. The discourse, or the assumptions, values, and worldview as they are embodied in communal practice, would encourage the client's appropriation of more functional beliefs, behaviors, and interpretive schemes.

While it is possible to give this Foucaultian account of therapeutic change in cognitive therapy, there are points of departure between Foucault and cognitive therapy. Foucault would disagree with the cognitive model about the mechanism of change. The cognitive model posits the individual as a relatively autonomous, rational being capable of making choices about which discourse will shape her perspective. By presenting rational arguments and behavioral evidence, the therapist reasons with the client and is able to demonstrate the superiority of functional beliefs and interpretive schemes. These functional schemes are more "objective" and correspond more completely to "reality" according to the cognitive model. We change in response to reason, we are free to choose alternative beliefs, interpretive schemes, automatic thoughts which better approximate the real world. Foucault would disagree with this Cartesian *cogito, ergo sum* view, the perspective that assumes the rational autonomous individual who is free to choose.

The individual in Foucault's view is the site of conflicting discourses, in a state of flux, constantly being constituted and reconstituted by competing discourses. Individuals in the modern world work, worship, consume, play, and vote in myriad discursive fields which compete for the constitution of the individual. Choice and rationality are not absent, but they are limited by the available discourses and their relative power. Foucault claims that individuals are constituted by discourses that are subtle and out of the realm of consciousness, and even less out of the realm of choice. The limits of Foucault's discursively constituted individual are inconsistent with the cognitive model's construal of the autonomous, rationally choosing client. Yet, in spite of this difference between cognitive therapy and Foucault, the two are not as disparate as they might seem. Foucault would maintain that a discursively constituted individual, while constrained in capacities for autonomous reason and choice, is not completely devoid of capacities for decision and agency. While this is certainly not identical to the assumptions of cognitive therapy, the two ways of thinking are compatible enough for the sake of this argument.

Conclusion

If pastors and pastoral counselors can be understood as bearers of discourse, bearers of a word of truth and hope and challenge that will call upon traditional Christian discourse, even constructed by the discourse ourselves, then a discursive analysis of pastoral counseling is appropriate. The analysis above is an attempt to articulate what pastors and counselors already do, as well as offer a challenge for doing it better.

As pastoral caregivers we use words, we lead institutions, we are enmeshed in ecclesiastical and psychological power relations. It is irresponsible to claim otherwise. If we call ourselves Christian, and if we claim to be formed personally and professionally by all that means, then we are inevitably part of the web of discourse called Christian scripture and tradition. Christian theology is discourse. It can no longer be seen as only a set of ideas or texts about God and the things of God. Rather theology is a part of a web of ideas, institutions, practices, psyches, bodies. How does theology function vis-à-vis women's psyches, and how does Christian theology reinforce, or do battle with, patriarchal truth-of-woman discourse? This is a critical question for those who care for depressed women.

Pastoral caregivers must examine the extent to which their theological language undergirds aspects of cultural stereotypes that foster depression in women. Theological descriptions of the human stance before God that emphasize helplessness, passivity, dependence, and self-emptying only reinforce depressogenic cultural notions of the ideal woman. How do our prayers, sermons, and pastoral care responses join the culture's view of women in upholding depressogenic attitudes? Furthermore, because depression is not only a matter of attitudes and beliefs, it is important that pastoral caregivers also be agents of social change, advocates for those with restricted access to power. Changing power relations within the church community, families, and in the social structures will have to be the province of pastoral caregivers who are intent on addressing the problem of women and depression.

Chapter Four

Self

The previous chapter took a wide angle view, looking at the relationship of social structures to depression in women. We considered a discursive web that includes institutions, bodies, psyches, language—one through which power circulates. This chapter begins with looking at the "self," taking a close-up view of depression in women. It is important to remember that the selves we respond to with care and compassion can never be separated from the social, political, economic contexts that shape them. Though we are turning from a theory of the way power functions in large social entities to psychologies concerned with the individual self, let us not forget that these selves are implicated at every turn in the power dynamics of larger structures.

The experience of depression for many is the experience of the absence of self. It is as though the self were gone, nowhere to be found. Feelings of love, hate, happiness, discontent, curiosity, attraction, interest, desire, and repulsion are absent. One looks inside and nothing is there. It feels as though one's self has disappeared, dissolved, dissipated. There may be a vague, deep sense of objectless dread, or a self-reproach for no discernable cause, yet nothing that one could call a true sense of self. Was the self never there to begin with? Is it there but hidden? Was it there but now it is gone forever? These questions emerge for the one seeking to understand the phenomenon of depression. While "recessed self" is not one of the clinically described symptoms of depression, one who has been depressed will recognize this as a distinctive and painful feature of depression.

Many feminist psychologists have described this experience in terms of loss and speak of a "loss of self."[1] Since Freud, loss has been named as a common trigger for depression. Usually the loss is described as a loss of a loved one, a job, a role, spouse, home, some valued feature of a life. Some feminist psychologists have said, yes, the trigger for depression is a loss, but not so much the loss of an external object, but rather the loss of self.

As mortal human beings, all women and men are vulnerable to all sorts of losses. Yet women are subject to a particular sort of loss that helps to account for the differences in rates of depression between women and men. The loss that triggers many women's depressions can be described as the loss of self. This can take the form of persistent erosion of self in conditions of belittling and trivialization. Or it can take the form of the failure to nurture and develop women's selves in the first place.[2] The systematic, chronic ignoring of a woman's feelings, thoughts, desires, and passions, an enterprise in which a woman herself may participate, can be understood as contributing to the loss of self. The truth-of-woman discourse discussed in the last chapter creates social and psychic space that for many women means a loss of self.

Another way to speak of what happens to women's selves is that they are "silenced."[3] Loss of self certainly expresses the experience of depression, and is an accurate description of a symptom, yet the loss is not irrevocable. Sexism renders women's selves hidden, clouded, thwarted, and damaged, but not altogether lost. The self is underground, or concealed, or rendered mute, not obliterated. In a Foucaultian language, this is evidence of resistance wherever there is power: the self persists, resists, in spite of destructive power structures. Affective disorders, unlike personality disorders, do not affect the structure of the self, nor do they destroy the self. They occlude or imprison the self, or anesthetize or stun-gun the self, but they do not destroy it. In fact, the one who has recovered from depression can give testimony to just how resilient the self is, just how irrepressible the self can be.[4] Therefore it is important that to the notion of a self lost we add the notion of a self silenced. "Self-silencing" carries the double meaning of the activity of silencing selves and the activity of silencing one's own self. Both senses are relevant to the dynamics of women's depression. Not only do outside factors conspire to silence women's selves, but also women silence themselves. The phenomenon of "internalizing the oppressor" is apparent in depressed women as they actively suppress feeling, desire, and agency.

A silenced self can be understood both as one feature of the *experience* of depression and as a *trigger* to depression. A self that feels inaccessible is clearly part of the experience of depression, but depression includes many other physiological and behavioral symptoms as well. Self-silencing is only one among many features of the experience of depression. Yet self-silencing functions also as a particularly important trigger to depression, the toxic condition for the beginnings of depression. It is as though the silencing of the self takes off and accumulates symptoms as it goes. One can imagine that habitual self-ignoring can begin to cascade down the hill in an avalanche, accumulating debris as it goes until it is the full-blown illness called depression.[5] Silencing the self is both cause and symptom of depression.

Self and Intimacy

What happens to women's selves in intimate relationships is critical to a full understanding of their depression. In Harriet Goldhor Lerner's discussion she addressed "female depression as it relates to a particular aspect of loss that occurs as women betray or sacrifice the self in order to preserve relationship harmony." She points out that "in attempting to navigate the delicate balance between the 'I' and the 'we,' women frequently sacrifice the 'I' in the service of togetherness, thus assuming a de-selfed position in relationships."[6]

She describes how some women believe they must choose between having a self and having a marriage.[7] They believe that asserting their desires, goals, or expectations, in short, their "selves," will necessarily alienate them from their mates. And since they also believe themselves to be inadequate, defenseless, and unlovable without a mate, an unacceptably painful condition, they choose to "de-self."[8] This self-betrayal, self-sacrifice, and self-negation is a source of depression. This belief is of course firmly grounded in cultural beliefs about women and in social practices expected of women, cultural beliefs characteristic of truth-of-woman discourse.

The erosion of self occurs as women shut themselves down, close themselves off to wellsprings of spirit and life and desire. This loss evokes grief. Dana Crowley Jack points to mourning the loss of self as responsible for depression in a great many women. She describes what "loss of self" means in three ways. First, it means the loss of voice in an intimate relationship. A woman ignores, denies, and considers irrelevant her own feelings, desires, or perspectives. She is silenced. Second, loss of self means fitting into others' view of who one should be, fulfilling others' expectations rather than one's own. Husband, parents, and the larger culture become the arbiters of who one is. Third, loss of self is manifest as continual negative self-labeling: they are right, I am wrong. Chronic self-blaming and doubting are characteristic of a loss of self.[9]

These three forms of loss of self can be self-imposed, self-administered, and self-policed, or they can be imposed by a violent or emotionally abusive partner.[10] The effect can be devastating. Ultimately, the self goes underground and provides a powerful trigger for an episode of depression.

Cognitive therapy enables a woman's rebellion against depression by helping her to assert selfhood even while under depression's tyranny. Cognitive therapy involves harnessing the power of the cognitive to begin to access the self, even though it is not accessible at an emotional, feeling level. Disciplining oneself to begin to think differently, question distorted thinking, and recognize cognitive errors that are symptomatic of depression is an assertion of the self in spite of the experience of its eclipse. It is as though the cognitive has access to the receded, hidden self. Behavioral aspects of cognitive therapy function in a similar way. Through an act of the will a depressed person can engage in palliative and healing activities that begin to coax the recessed self out of hiding. Cognitive-behavioral interventions, as discussed in chapter 2, are ways of subverting oppressive discourses and making possible the emergence of healthier ones that create subject positions better for women. The following case study illustrates a course of pastoral counseling where I, the therapist, approached a woman's depression as an eclipsed, hidden self. I used several cognitive therapy techniques to gently coax her to find and assert the hidden, recessed self.

Case Study: Sally

Sally was a young single woman in her early thirties who came to see me for pastoral counseling because she believed she was depressed. She spoke Japanese and had just started working for a multinational corporation that valued her language skills immensely and rewarded her very well financially. Her job included supervising a staff of eleven, mostly men. She felt too new to the job to feel confident in her skills. She had replaced a man thirty years her senior and was not sure of her staff's perception of her as a leader. She often felt their lack of trust in her authority. And she often felt empty, overwhelmed, spent, and lost. Her boyfriend of two years, Ron, was beginning to complain about never seeing her, and this was a source of distress to her. Lately all she wanted to do was sleep. She had gained weight and felt distracted and tired all the time. She felt like she was just going through the motions of her work, even though it was a job that she had worked hard to get. I agreed with her that she did indeed sound depressed, and that we should focus on that first.

I referred her to a psychiatrist so that she could begin taking antidepressant medication. Sally had some resistance to this suggestion because she felt she should be able to "work this out" by herself. I explained that some people are biologically more vulnerable to depression than others, and that from time to time an antidepressant is useful. The analogy of diabetes was helpful for her, and allowed her to see the medication in the same category as insulin.

After a few sessions, several patterns became clear. First of all, the Daily Activities Schedule that Sally had been keeping revealed that there were few activities in her life that gave her a sense of either "mastery" or "pleasure." She still felt new at her job and gained little sense of competence there. During the evening she watched TV and recuperated from the day. Weekends were spent with her boyfriend, who emerged as quite demanding. He insisted that they spend both Saturday and Sunday together, even though he was often consumed by sports on TV. So her pleasurable activities were quite few. We discussed ways to increase her mastery and pleasure activities. Seeing other friends, spending some weekend time alone reading, and playing tennis twice a week added to her pleasurable activities. I also recommended a morning workout at the health club at work.

Second, the Dysfunctional Thought Record showed thoughts that were characteristically associated with her depressed mood. "He thinks I am stupid." "I am a terrible supervisor." "I look ugly and haggard." "I sounded too demanding and harsh." I helped Sally develop some responses to these thoughts, such as finding alternative explanations for a coworker's puzzled look—he might be just as tired as she is. No, she is not a terrible supervisor, even as a new one, she is able to lead adequately, and shows promise of improving soon. It was important to quickly give her cognitive and behavioral techniques that could begin to provide some symptom relief.

When Sally's automatic thoughts were pressed, they all pointed to her certainty that she would never be in a satisfying love relationship. Her beliefs showed a double bind: if she is a failure at work, no man will want her; if she is a success at work, no man will want her. As a failure, she is, after all, a loser, and what man wants a loser? As a professional success, she will alienate and threaten her peers. Therefore, she was caught in a situation where she could not win, because both her successes and her failures bore the meaning, "alone for the rest of my life."

We began to talk more about her relationship with Ron. It became clearer to me that he was emotionally needy and therefore very controlling. Sally felt reluctant to disagree with him and was fearful of his anger. She often dreaded the weekends with him, but felt that he really did love her. When I asked why she did not date other men, she said that she was afraid Ron would fall apart without her, and that there were no other men out there anyway.

Many aspects of Sally's relationship with Ron were congruent with Jack's description of a silenced self. She kept her opinions to herself, preferring harmony to his angry outbursts. She did not pursue friendships with others nor other interests because her job and her relationship were so consuming. Her world was becoming smaller and smaller as she tried to live on the terms set by her job and by Ron. The result was depression. The situation in life in which Sally ignored her self was the trigger to an episode of depression.

The relationship with Ron was difficult to deal with therapeutically. So much in her background, and so much in the culture, told her that first of all, her worth was found in a relationship with a man, and second, she had better maintain relationship harmony or else.

So I helped Sally build up a sense of self. I began by helping her recall a time when she had a greater access to her self. What was that like? What was she doing in her life? She spoke of her friends, work, family. I helped her visualize that time, her image of herself then, and what it felt like. What was missing now? What can change? She started looking more closely at her relationship with Ron. She said he loved her, but how did she feel? How did she feel when she was with him? At one point, she looked very tired, and said simply, "drained."

She began to seek out other friends and activities, and learned to recognize her feelings with Ron, instead of only focusing on his. Sally also began to get some distance from her work. Her work continued to be very important to her, but she realized she had become too merged with the job, and needed to remember what had led her to that position in the first place. She remembered her love for Japanese language and art, and began to include the cultural side of her job in her daily activities, as well as the number crunching. She also identified several co-workers whose opinion of her she had overinflated, and began to evaluate her work herself, rather than relying only on their rather critical opinions. Over the months, as Sally began to reconnect with and to assert her self, the depression lifted slowly. She became a much happier, healthier woman.

Self and Work

The example of Sally helps us to see beyond interpersonal relationships as the only relevant factor in the well-being of women's selves. In addition to events in intimate relationships, family, and friendships, a woman's work is also important to her sense of self. Engaging in a meaningful vocation, and one that provides a sense of competence and economic independence, has a great deal of impact on a woman's mental health. In fact, one study shows that, if a woman could choose either a happy marriage or a low-stress job, she would be at a lower risk of depression if she chose the job.[11]

Fortunately, we are beyond the early days of feminism when "work" was romanticized as the solution for bored, depressed, understimulated, middle-class, suburban, white women. We now know that, for many poor women, work is not for personal fulfillment, but for their survival and that of their children. Poor women have always worked, and often in underpaid, unsatisfying jobs. Work itself is not the answer. What is required is a certain kind of work: one that draws on talents and passions, is paid justly, offers child care and freedom from sexual harassment and chronic belittling.

In the case of Sally, had I focused only on her self in interpersonal terms, I would have missed an important part of her life. Not only did her job consume the greatest number of hours of her week, but also it was a way she had chosen to develop, as a competent leader in the business world. Enhancing a woman's meaningful work life, encouraging a sense of vocation, and developing her sense of entitlement to it, is a very important part of attention to the self that the care of depressed women requires.

The Pastoral Counseling of Women's Selves

Often our theology hinders us in pastoral counseling of the woman whose self is silenced. We can appeal to God's care for each individual, to God as the shepherd who leaves the ninety-nine for the sake of the one, and as the woman who searches for the lost coin until she finds it, and recognize that we are each created in the image of God. Yet we have overwhelming messages in our tradition that love for self, care for self, especially if it means asking for something, is wrong. A "de-selfed" position seems to be, on the surface of things, what our tradition declares is the highest good. Our challenge as pastoral caregivers is to find strands in our heritage that encourage a woman to speak her voice, feel the fullness of her emotions, and act with conviction and self-love on her own behalf.

Fortunately, we do have rich theological resources at our disposal in the task of nurturing a woman's meaningful work life. We can speak of the importance of call, referring to the call narratives of the prophets, who protested their inadequacy, yet still responded, "Here am I, send me." Jesus' call to his disciples, inviting them to follow him, is compelling imagery for one struggling with vocation. Paul's conversion experience has been reinterpreted from an experience of forgiven guilt to an experience of call and vocation. Fundamental to an experience of Jesus Christ is the summons to a particular work. While not all women can express their call in the work for which they are paid, they can be encouraged to discern a call and to find avenues for fulfilling it.

The Socially Constructed Self

We have discussed the impact of both interpersonal and vocational life on the self, and how silencing in either realm can be a trigger to depression. Yet in discussing the self, we must be aware that there are differences of opinion regarding what the self is in the first place, or if it even exists. The dominant view in the modern West has been that the self is a separate, autonomous, choosing entity that can opt for or against intimacy, can control the environment and its resources for personal gain, and can affiliate with community if it meets one's needs. One writer described the Western view of the self as "a bounded, unique, singular, encapsulated, noncorporeal, ghostlike, and godly entity."[12]

Feminists and members of other cultures point out an alternative view: "To the extent that one is or has a self at all, this self is seen as constituted by social interactions, contexts and relationships."[13] They point out that the very notion of selfhood is culturally bound. In many cultures, awareness of social role and responsibility far outweighs awareness of the self and its inner contours. From this perspective it is impossible to view individuals apart from context and from their communities. The self is inextricable from the context of culture, power, community, and tradition. I expressed this alternative view in chapter 3 by speaking of the role of discourse in constituting a self, by speaking of individuals as constituted by a web of not only interpersonal relationships but also ideas, power arrangements, institutions, and so forth. Individuals become the site of the contest of discourses, power-laden formations, competing to construct them as subjects. In the case of Sally, we can imagine that she was constructed by truth-of-woman discourse, business management discourse, a discourse with space for other cultures, and a discourse with space for women in positions of power. These discourses compete to construct her as a subject.

Not only are there cultural differences in the view of the self, but there are also important philosophical differences. One way to describe the debate is in terms of the distinction between modern and postmodern views. Modernism conceives of a unitary, autonomous, self-contained subject, or self, capable of free choice and objective rationality. Postmodern writers, on the other hand, have proclaimed the "death of the subject," the end of the time when one can speak meaningfully of a discrete entity called self.[15] The boundaries between individual and language and strategies of power blur. Postmodern thinking tends to dissolve the subject, or self, to render it the passive construct of suprapersonal forces beyond any individual or even class control. This analysis performs the important function of calling attention to the embeddedness of all people in a social/political/economic context. We are reminded of the critical importance of changing social structures if we are to affect the lives of those to whom we give care.

The problem with this view of the subject as simply a social construct is that it is not a way of speaking that empowers. Proclaiming the death of the subject hardly inspires the kind of persistent commitment to social justice that recalcitrant corporate structures require if they are to be corrected. Nancy Hartsock makes the now familiar but important point when she asks, "Why is it that just at the moment when so many of us who have been silenced begin to demand the right to name ourselves, to act as subjects rather than objects of history, that just then the concept of subjecthood becomes problematic?"[15]

In addition, it is not helpful therapeutically to conceive of a suffering person, or to speak to a suffering person, with the assumption that the subject, the self, is a node where discourses intersect. First of all, self-as-node language disables the pastoral counselor from engaging in deep, compassionate empathy. Empathetic with what? or whom? we might ask. Second, it is language that confirms depressed persons' worst fears about themselves: there is nothing there. The painful journey toward health is hardly funded by assumptions that there is really no one there.

Foucault did not always refer to the subject in the same way. Later in his writing he moves from what could be seen as a passively constructed subject who is an empty space where discourses intersect, to an understanding of subjects who play a role in their own construction. He describes his later project as concerned with "the way a human being turns him- or herself into a subject."[16] It is here that Foucault becomes especially helpful. While his earlier work highlights the profound impact of social location and the dangers of making universal claims, his later work makes it easier to speak of an individual actively engaged in constructing a life and a place in the world.

I prefer to think of the self, or subject, as a "subject-in-process," following Julia Kristeva.[17] According to Kristeva, "We are subjects *in process*, ceaselessly losing our identity, destabilized by fluctuations in our relations to the other, to whom we nevertheless remain bound by a kind of homeostasis."[18] She also refers to the "provisional unity" of the subject, again calling attention to the changing, yet not disintegrating, subject.[19] In a discussion of Kristeva's psychoanalytic practice, Toril Moi describes Kristeva's understanding of "an unstable and always threatened, yet nevertheless real and necessary, form of subjectivity."[20]

> The analyst is after all engaged in the task of healing her patients, and has therefore to provide them with some kind of "identity" which will enable them to live in the world. . . . [W]ithout some kind of subject structure, meaningful, subversive or creative action is impossible. . . . The modern, unstable and empty subject, she argues, ought not to be fixed and stabilized, but to be turned into a *work in progress.*[21]

Conceiving of someone for whom we care as a "work in progress" enables counselors to understand both the fluidity of clients' selves and some sort of recognizable identity. We can name the multiple social, political, and economic forces that are continually forming our clients and parishioners, while caring for a person with some singularity. It gives people a way to understand the openness of the future: they are not bound by what has been, nor are they bound by the current arrangement of things. It empowers women to assume the position of agent, of an actor capable of shaping the course of her life. The self as work-in-progress is neither static nor substantive, yet it is *something*, it does suggest a referent for the word "self."

The view of the subject as work-in-progress, as something fluid and always being created and recreated, does not mean that we can leave the modernist language of "self" behind. In spite of philosophical reasons to avoid the term "self," which suggests a static and fully autonomous unit, the language of self is still important for one very important reason: it works therapeutically. Therefore, throughout this book I consistently speak of depression in terms of what happens to women's selves in patriarchal social arrangements: I refer to self-silencing and the eclipse of the self; I describe the therapeutic process as encouraging a woman to claim selfhood, to know and to assert self. This use of self-language clearly suggests a unitary, substantial entity that is hushed or eclipsed in depression, and is either given a voice or found for the first time in psychotherapy. Though this view is inconsistent with the use of Foucault, and even with Kristeva's self as work-in-progress, it is very effective language for women seeking to heal from depression. It is my experience that the language of self—of true self, authentic self, hidden-but-emerging self, lost-but-found self—is very therapeutically empowering for women.

Why is this the case? The answer lies in recognizing the damage done to women in a culture where things female have been rendered invisible, derivative, or frivolous. In this context the language of the self, a substantial and choosing self with boundaries, supports a woman's agency and helps her make important changes, expect respect for boundaries of body and soul, and act with a sense of entitlement to meaningful love and work. It is possible that this modern category, self, is effective because most of us adult women have been socially constructed by modernist discourse: self language works therapeutically because it is the language that made us.[22] In modern discourse, it has been the white male subject, of course, that has had the greater opportunity to at least approximate the choosing, autonomous subject, objectively naming truth and reality, harnessing and subduing the natural world. Women have been excluded from this process in the social-political constellations of modernity. So when women hear this language, heavy with modern overtones, as including them as women, it sounds like emancipatory good news. It is the task of the therapist, the theologian, the pastoral caregiver, to transform the modern understanding of "self" into something resembling the postmodern understanding of "work-in-progress" that is deeply connected to social systems, for better or worse. It is our responsibility to "redeem" self language, at least in this interim between the modern and the postmodern. Most of us are deeply inscribed with modernist categories for thinking about ourselves, and it is not clear that there has yet emerged a postmodern language of an accountable moral agent, a subject position that allows for both self-love and love of others. We use the language we have, until better categories come along.

Sylvia Plath's *The Bell Jar* helps to illustrate the way postmodernist language of "discursively constructed subject" can be used in conjunction with modernist language of "self."[23] This semiautobiographical novel powerfully illustrates the event of depression as an event of the self, and how discourse plays a major role in the self's well-being. Plath's account of her depression can be read as an account of truth-of-woman discourse and how resistance discourse can "do battle" with it. This book can be read as an illustration of contesting discourses at the site of a woman's self.[24]

The Bell Jar

Esther Greenwood, the central character in *The Bell Jar*, was spending the summer working at *Ladies' Day* magazine offices in New York City. She and several other college women had been selected for the honor of serving as guest editors of the annual college issue of the magazine. They all lived on the same hall in a comfortable New York hotel and, in addition to their editing and writing work at the magazine, attended various parties and luncheons appropriate for young ladies in the 1950s.

"Doubleness, Smiles, and Compromise"

Early in the narrative there is an incident that illustrates the self-silencing of women's depression. Esther and her friend Doreen met a couple of guys, and the foursome went to a bar together. Though the meeting showed promise at first, it quickly became clear that the more desirable of the two men was interested in Doreen, while Esther considered the other man to be socially pathetic. In this awkward social situation Esther makes several statements about her sense of herself. "I felt myself melting into the shadows like the negative of a person I'd never seen before. . . . I felt myself shrinking to a small black dot against all those red and white rugs and that pine paneling. I felt like a hole in the ground."[25] And upon returning home, "The silence depressed me. It wasn't the silence of silence. It was my own silence."[26] Though she was alive and awake and somewhat participatory in the situation, she had a sense of inner absence, vacuity, a loss of self or estrangement from a familiar and recognizable self. Melting, a negative, shrinking, small black dot, a hole, silence . . . these are the metaphors she uses to speak of a progressively receding, silenced self. The social situation in which she is not chosen by the most desirable man evokes a sense of shrinking and silence.

What precisely is responsible for her shrinking, silenced self? During the course of the evening Esther noted a moment of awareness of the disparity

between inner world and outer appearance: "Even when they [things] surprised me or [made] me sick I never let on, but pretended that's the way I
knew things were all the time."[27] The diminishing selfhood involved in depression began with an incongruity between feelings and behavior. The social pressure on Esther to live up to standards of femininity at the expense
of congruency between self and behavior is the beginning of the loss of self
that she experiences here.

Dana Crowley Jack's account of woman's double life is relevant here. An
inner life, the authentic I, is repressed and suppressed, while the outer self
performs in acceptable conformity to a feminine ideal. Is this the beginning
of the pathology of depression? At one point Esther speaks of "year after year
of doubleness and smiles and compromise."[28] This phrase reminds us of Foucault's notion of power in the interstices, the imposition of doubleness,
smiles, and compromise that truth-of-woman discourse imposes on the interstitial level, the level of individual women's psyches. Here the cause of depression, self-silencing imposed by dominant discourse, coincides with a
symptom of depression, an inaccessible self. The experience of a receding and
absent self that is the experience of depression coalesces with cultural pressures for women to deny self for the sake of living up to the feminine ideal.

The incident also speaks of Esther's perception of her body. In speaking
of her being taller than the pathetic man, she spoke of feeling "gawky and
morbid as somebody in a sideshow."[29] It was not acceptable to be a tall
woman, or at least a woman taller than her date. Later she saw her reflection and was "appalled to see how wrinkled and used up I looked."[30] Her
interpretive lens for her body is clearly derogatory. Then she does a very
interesting thing, which seems to be an act of reclaiming her body. She decided to take a very hot bath, because "There must be quite a few things a
hot bath won't cure, but I don't know many of them."[31] At this point early
in her depression, the bodily immersion in a hot bath was still able to function as palliative and healing. "I never feel so much myself as when I'm in
a hot bath."[32] It is as though the self that had disappeared before was restored as she immerses her body in the bath. She notes, "I felt myself growing pure again."[33] Images of birth, rebirth, and babies appear. "I don't
believe in baptism or the waters of Jordan or anything like that, but I guess
I feel about a hot bath the way those religious people feel about holy water
. . . , and when I stepped out at last . . . I felt pure and sweet as a new baby."[34]
Clearly, a reclamation of her body was a reclamation of her self.

Self as Object of Reproach

In a later incident, we see a critique of traditional standards of femininity,
standards that we can understand as the truth-of-woman discourse that in-

cludes ideas, images, and moral standards as well as concrete power relations. During one of the luncheons planned for the visiting guest editors, they were greeted as "the prettiest, smartest bunch of young ladies our staff has yet had the good luck to meet."[35] The luncheon was a demonstration of the magazine's "Food Testing Kitchens."[36] At one point during this most trivial of presentations, Esther turned to her neighbor, Betsy, who had been described as "straight from Kansas with her bouncing blonde ponytail and Sweetheart-of-Sigma-Chi smile," and asked her how another planned event, the fur show, had been.[37] "'It was wonderful,' Betsy smiled. 'They showed us how to make an all-purpose neckerchief out of mink tails and a gold chain. . . . '"[38] Clearly Plath is critiquing the standards of femininity that the young women were being groomed for.

As the bouncing blonde continues the inane description of the trivial, thrifty adornments they were taught to make, Esther pondered the fact that she missed another friend who would have "murmured some fine, scalding remark about [the] miraculous furpiece to cheer me up," as though the friend could have somehow deconstructed the absurd patriarchal discourse of womanhood with a sarcastic comment.[39] The "fine, scalding remark" could have functioned as resistance discourse in the interstitial spaces of the ridiculous luncheon. However, because she had been unable to give voice to how ridiculous the luncheon and fur show were, her mood sinks, and she begins to have painful, negative automatic thoughts, in the cognitive therapy sense, regarding herself and her future.

> I felt very low. I had been unmasked only that morning by Jay Cee [her boss] herself, and I felt now that all the uncomfortable suspicions I had about myself were coming true, and I couldn't hide the truth much longer. After nineteen years of running after good marks and prizes and grants of one sort and another, I was letting up, slowing down, dropping clean out of the race.[40]

These ruminations about her future are clearly examples of the kinds of distorted thoughts that accompany depression. We can see the convergence of events: as the absurdity of the '50s feminine milieu reaches its height, her mood plummets, and her thoughts turn to self-criticism. Rather than the object of her scorn continuing to be the external, sexist inanities, she has turned her reproach against herself. She turns the critique against herself, believing her life has been a sham, and that the truth about her inadequacies was on the verge of being made public. Unable to fully unmask or critique the oppressive discourse around her, she instead considers herself unmasked, proven to be a sham, a fake. Having no resistance discourse at her disposal, and in the absence of her friend Doreen, the bearer of resistance discourse, she turns the deconstruction against herself and her accomplishments.

Inside the Bell Jar

Following a suicide attempt later in the book, Esther is hospitalized. When a wealthy woman patron of the arts, Mrs. Guinea, offers to finance her recovery, Esther is moved to an expensive residential hospital for treatment. As she is driven to the new place, she crosses a bridge and schemes a jump from the car and into the waters below. At this point comes one of the most poignant paragraphs in the book, one that summarizes the inner death involved in depression, the sense of no feelings, loss of interest and capacity for pleasure, and a sense of inner malignancy or decay.

> I knew I should be grateful to Mrs. Guinea, only I couldn't feel a thing. If Mrs. Guinea had given me a ticket to Europe, or a round-the-world cruise, it wouldn't have made one scrap of difference to me, because wherever I sat—on the deck of a ship or at a street café in Paris or Bangkok—I would be sitting under the same glass bell jar, stewing in my own sour air.[41]

For the first time she refers to the title of the book, the bell jar. In this context it seems to be a metaphor for being locked inside her kingdom of depression with its putrefaction, rot, decay, and stagnant air. As the ride continues, "I sank back in the gray, plush seat and closed my eyes. The air of the bell jar wadded round me and I couldn't stir."[42]

It seems to me that being trapped in a bell jar is like being trapped in a discourse, or in cognitive therapy terms, trapped in distorting schemes. Just as the curves of the bell jar twist and distort the perception of the one looking out, so do depressogenic schemes warp the depressed person's view. And, from a Foucaultian perspective, we can see the added dimension of a discursive formation, which constructs a subject position where only certain truths are possible. Just as a bell jar creates a position with its truth, so does a discursive formation construct a position where only certain things count as true. In the case of depressed women, these truths are misogynist views of women as incompetent, less valuable than men, not created in the image of God, etc. In a bell jar a person is there but not there, close yet utterly separate, visible yet silent, on display yet alone. The bell jar defines what its occupant will see, experience, and count as true, just as schemata and discourses do.

As the narrative progresses, Esther meets a therapist, Dr. Nolan, who makes a dramatic difference in her life. In the course of their relationship, Esther recovers a sense of self and life.

At one point, Esther is very reluctantly taken to receive electroconvulsive shock treatment. Afterward, she describes how she felt much better.

> All the heat and fear purged itself. I felt surprisingly at peace. The bell jar hung, suspended, a few feet above my head. I was open to the circulating air.[43]

Yet the last reference to a bell jar is ominous.

> How did I know that someday—at college, in Europe, somewhere, any-
> where—the bell jar, with its stifling distortions, wouldn't descend again? [44]

The person who has been depressed knows the dread of its return, the powerlessness over its appearance, and the fear that the reliability of the world,
the self, the future, the network of relationships, may again be ripped apart.
She refers to the distortions of the bell jar, the fact that the world, the self,
and so on, are twisted, warped, rendered horrors.

As the young woman's self appeared, the bell jar lifted, and she was reborn. Yet, even as Esther is reborn, Plath strikes an ominous note in her
suggestions that the bell jar could be lowered at any time. We are reminded
of the fragility of Esther's sense of self in an environment that remains hostile to the emergence of women's selves.

The Bell Jar gives a useful illustration not only of the dark world of the
depressed, but also a way of talking about how discourse can function to silence the self, rendering women depressed, and how resistance discourse
functions to aid the rebellion against it.

Conclusion

This chapter on the self is situated between one devoted to social location and one devoted to relationship. It is difficult to discuss the self apart
from the impact of social context and interpersonal matrices. In order to
understand depression in women, and to help women to overcome it, we
must attend to several loci: social location, the self, relationship, and (as we
will discuss in chapter 6) the body. All are connected; each plays a vital role
in the genesis of depression in women and in disrupting its hold on women.
In order to have a full theological understanding, each of these loci must be
considered. In other words, the justice issues raised by a consideration of
social location, and the challenges to a view of love for God and other as
self-negation, apply to each chapter. These challenges are discussed further
in the next chapter, devoted to exploring what happens to women's selves
in relationships.

Chapter Five

Relationship

I think . . . that women desire . . . places of inner and outer freedom in which new forms of connection *can take place. Liberated from relational bondage, we range through an unlimited array of relations—not just to other persons, but to ideas and feelings, to the earth, the body, and the untold contents of the present moment. In other words, women struggling against the constraints of conventionally feminine modes of relation desire not less but more (and different) relation; not disconnection, but* connection that counts.

—*Catherine Keller*[1]

Catherine Keller refers to "women's traditional specialization in relationship." This "specialization" has been recognized by many and attributed to everything from biology to culture, from essence to social construct, from nature to nurture, from pathology to health, from God's will to the devil's doing. However it is accounted for, this tendency seems to be a fact of gendered life in most places.[2] What is interesting is how this tendency is evaluated in traditional psychology. The female tendency toward relationship has been called an unhealthy "dependency" by many in the field of psychology and blamed as a source of depression. The desire for connection is seen as a pathological need to be attached to another in order to parasitically derive self-esteem, purpose, or identity. It is a sign of an undeveloped ego that requires a significant object for a sense of wholeness.

Some writers in feminist psychology of women challenge this view of women's relationality. They locate this relational tendency not in stilted development, or a poorly developed self, but rather in the different developmental process for girls and women. Nancy Chodorow describes how traditional parenting practices give rise to a path from childhood to adulthood that is different for girls than boys. In traditional pattern, the mother is primarily responsible for child rearing, and the father is the emotionally distant and dominant presence in the family. In order to become an adult, the (male) boy must separate from the (female) mother and assume the father's dominant role in family and society.

On the other hand, for the (female) girl to become an adult, separation from the (female) mother is not the critical movement, rather it is the search for a new form of relatedness within the ongoing relationship with the mother. Therefore boys separate from the primary caregiver, while girls continue the connection in a new way. For girls, differentiation does not equal separation, but rather an assertion of one's agency within the relationship. Carol Gilligan's work on adolescent girls' development demonstrates that development is hampered when a girl is unable to remain connected and, at the same time, form a distinct self within the relationship.[3]

Feminist psychologists point out that the resulting relationship orientation, far from being a hindrance to women's mental health, in fact protects women from depression. For example, clinical studies show that the increased ability to experience and communicate feelings of sadness is clearly a protecting factor.[4] This capacity has a cathartic effect and also enlists social support. Lerner addresses this erroneous assumption that high affiliative needs render women vulnerable to depression. She claims, to the contrary, that being relationship-oriented can only be understood as a healthy quality, not a weakness that leaves one vulnerable to pathology. Therefore, Lerner concludes, "the primary valuing of relationships (when relatedness does not occur at the expense of self) is part of the solution, not the problem."[5]

It is not relationality that is the problem, rather, it is the patriarchal form of many interpersonal relationships that is the problem. Lerner claims the problem is "what *happens* to women in relationships," not women's orientation to relationship.[6] She points to the subordination of women in traditional marriages, the economic dependence of many married women, divorce as the only recourse society offers to a stifling marriage, and gender roles of passivity, dependence, and helplessness, all of which lend themselves to the depressogenic nature of many traditional relationships.

Women's healthy desire for relationship is continually frustrated by both a woman's belief that she is not entitled to intimacy and her partner's failure to connect on an intimate level. Dana Crowley Jack claims that the ensuing healthy yearning for closeness is then often interpreted as pathological dependence, or neediness. Unhealthy dependence is not the problem, rather, the problem is a woman's failure to strongly assert her intimacy needs and/or her partner's failure to meet them. Jack draws on Bowlby to claim that attachment is not a sign of unhealthy dependence but that it is healthy and necessary for the development of a self. If traditional theories have named the inability to let go of a loved object, for example, a loss of a relationship, as responsible for depression, Jack claims that it is the loss of self within an ongoing relationship that causes women's depression. "Depression is precipitated . . . by the recognition that they have lost themselves in trying to establish an intimacy that was never attained."[7] Therefore the hopelessness and helplessness in depression has to do with the possibility of bringing their full selfhood, with its desires, needs, and assertions, into intimate relationship.

According to Jack, whether or not depressed women are seen as pathologically dependent is based on two different understandings of the self: *the separate self* and *the relational self*. She claims Freud is characteristic of the individualist view that the healthy self is autonomous and independent, unchanged by relationships. Jack sees Freud as claiming that depression is a result of a failure to separate, an inability to properly detach from a loved object. By contrast, Jack sees the healthy self as fundamentally based on a matrix of relationships. She claims that connectedness forms the very foundation of the self. Therefore, to understand depression, one must not look to the intrapsychic defect of the failure to individuate, but to what is happening in interpersonal networks.

Therefore, to understand the source of a woman's depression, one must not search for the pathologically dependent traits of her individual psyche; rather, one must examine the matrix of relationships in which she is embedded that have engendered a loss of self.

A word of critique is in order at this point. Is it not possible to speak of the self as both separate and relational? While Jack recognizes that autonomy is of critical importance, for her any autonomy is always a subset of relatedness. In the context of depression it is critical to speak of a self that survives when relational webs are inaccessible. During an episode of depression, when the capacity for relationality is virtually absent, it is the lone, durable, and resilient self that can survive the ravages of depression. Insisting that the self is a subset of relationality does not take into account the endurance of those who have survived the profound isolation of depression. While supportive, intimate relationships are extremely helpful in surviving depression, it is the individual, resilient self that endures. Autonomy plays an important role in both protection from and survival of depression.

The focus on relationship requires an additional cautionary note. The linkage between relationality and women can perpetuate nineteenth-century notions of the public-private split, with women belonging to the sphere of the private, which includes relational spheres such as family harmony and emotional well-being. Rather than adding yet another voice calling for women to be the "keeper of the relationships" in the private, domestic realm, there needs to be a call for women to develop a voice in the public realm. This can include experiencing efficacy as an organizer of women and working directly on public issues affecting all women, actively engaged in changing patriarchal structures, as Greenspan has described it.

More importantly, developing a voice in the public realm may mean developing a sense of self in the realm of work, as discussed in chapter 4. Developing a vocation, a call, may be just as important as developing a self in interpersonal relationship. It may be that the development of the self that is possible in vocational development is the critical element. Women are already relationally oriented and often need little coaxing to give attention to this realm. It is the development of gifts, skills, talents, vocational identity, or making a public contribution to the larger community in the form of work that may be the critical factor in claiming selfhood. While many feminist women speak of the importance of developing skills and creativity, these are often seen as secondary to the interpersonal realm. While relationship is a very important issue in the discussion of depressed women, there are other vital issues to be considered as well.

Case Study: Marcy

Marcy came to the pastoral counseling center with a vague sense of something wrong in her life. She would often describe her life with a smile and a laugh, and with tears in her eyes. She would fall silent, weeping soundlessly. Yet she was unable to say exactly what was wrong.

"I love my husband, we have a nice home, though I can't keep it clean (laugh), my children are so precious to me, . . . but I feel so empty inside. Hollow. Like there is no me anywhere. I don't even know what I think about anything anymore. And I have to control my temper."

Marcy was in her early thirties, married to a man seeking to progress in his banking career, with two pre-school-age daughters. She worked as a computer programmer one day a week and visited her grandmother several times a week in a nearby nursing home. Her life was mostly consumed with household duties and children, yet she was in a generation of women who grew up hearing the rhetoric of the women's movement about professional success, independence, and self-fulfillment. She seemed to be apologizing for the course her life had taken, as though she didn't really know how this happened to her. Also part of her discourse was the language of faith. She was active in her church, prayed regularly, and was conscientious about helping others in the church community as well as sensitive to larger issues in the world. She felt she should be grateful for all she had, and that she should do more, and she shouldn't be so preoccupied with herself and her own happiness. She felt guilty for being unhappy, and for seeking help.

Our first conversations were about how she never had time to do anything well: neither her housekeeping, nor care for her children or grandmother, nor participation in church activities, nor developing her work life. Things were always kept dangling and unfinished. Strangely absent was talk of her husband. I began to wonder about this. When we first began talking, I gave Marcy an open-ended opportunity to "tell me about your husband." She said he was a wonderful person, not perfect, but a good husband and father. There was little emotion in her voice, and her eyes were blank. On the other hand, when she spoke of her youngest daughter, her eyes sparkled with tears as she described her deep love and devotion to her.

Marcy often felt tired, took naps whenever she could, and had trouble staying on any one task. She and her husband rarely had sex anymore because "the girls might hear," and because she had "become enormous." She had gained thirty pounds in the past year, and she felt very unattractive and undisciplined. She even spoke of her weight gain as a spiritual failure.

Eventually it became clear to me that Marcy was moderately depressed. She was able to carry out her responsibilities, and able to feel some emotion in respect to her children, but other topics evoked little genuine affect. Her physical symptoms, fatigue, loss of libido, change in appetite, and change in sleep patterns all pointed to depression.

When I asked Marcy what she did to nurture herself, she did not understand the question. She thought I was referring to a balanced, nutritious diet. I smiled and rephrased the question as, What do you do to take care of your own needs? "Oh I know on the talk shows they always talk about taking care of yourself, and I should take care of myself, I know I should, but I just don't have time." Rather than argue with her, I chose not to add one more critical voice that said, "You are inadequate because you are failing to take care of yourself." I simply posed the question again. "How do you feed your soul, your spirit?" Immediately her eyes welled up with tears. I asked what she was feeling. She said she had forgotten that she had a spirit. "And you are feeling . . . ?" "Sad," she said, "very, very sad."

"Can you remember a time when you knew you had a spirit?"

Marcy then began to talk about a time in her life when her spirit was very much alive. She spoke of her early career that included travel and friends. Things were not perfect then. The hours were long, and she often felt lonely on the work trips, and her relationship with her parents was rocky. But she said she felt strong, adventurous, attractive, and lively. Though she had grown up in the church, she was not active then, because she was either traveling or recovering from working hard or playing hard.

I asked her what happened to that strong, vivacious person, to that spirited woman. She said she didn't know, but that it was amazing to remember her. She felt like an entirely different person now, and she had forgotten the former self.

Since Marcy was comfortable with the language of spirit, I wondered out loud about her spirit and the Spirit of God. She responded that she felt spiritually negligent, and she knew if she prayed more, attended Sunday school, controlled her temper, and was able to follow through on church projects, that she would feel more spiritually alive. I sensed a contradiction. Marcy felt spirited when she was independent, but she described personal piety, self-giving, and self-control as the route to greater spirituality. In her prayer life she tried to listen to God instead of to herself, to get herself "out of the way" so that she could do God's will, and not her own. She believed her problems stemmed from listening to herself, and not to God. Her theological script for spiritual well-being seemed to be self-emptying prayer, self-sacrifice for family and church, and self-control when she felt such troublesome feelings as frustration or anger. Her God was "out there," separate from the deep needs and desires of the self.[8]

It seemed that God required the same self-silencing as the culture. God and patriarchy were in an unholy alliance to render her mute. I soon found that her husband was part of the alliance as well.

It seemed clear to me that some marital counseling would be in order. So, I invited Marcy's husband Roland in for a session with both of them. A first impression of Roland was that he was thoughtful and bright. He seemed to have a studied casualness about him, in other words, his informality seemed a little planned. He expressed his concern for Marcy, and said that he wanted to do whatever it took to help her feel better about herself. Marcy smiled and laughed more than usual, but said less than usual. He usually addressed me, and rarely her. His underlying agenda of the session seemed to be, "let's get Marcy fixed," and she seemed to go along.

They came to the third session together looking tense. She looked miserable, he looked grim. Roland wanted to have an office Christmas party at their house, but felt the house was too untidy for entertaining. Marcy did not see how she could have a large party and do all the other Christmas preparations for her family and at church. I was internally relieved that a conflict had arisen, because they had been so agreeable before. My agenda for the session was not to work out the problem of the Christmas party, but to see if they could each articulate their own feelings, as well as hear and articulate the other's.

I asked Roland to explain, at a feeling level, the importance of the party. He said that they had not done much socially since Marcy had been "down," and he wanted that to be a part of their life. Furthermore, the party was important for his professional advancement. When I asked Marcy if she could tell Roland the feelings she heard, she quickly articulated his feeling of frustration over their social isolation, as well as his desire to progress in his company. Then Marcy explained her feelings of being overwhelmed by the demands of the holiday season, and her feeling inadequate to any of the tasks, much less adding another one, and her fear of disappointing him. Then I asked Roland to tell Marcy the feelings he heard. His response was classic. His first response was to argue that yes, it was possible for her to get it all done. Then he restated his deep desire for the party. Then he suggested that it was because of her that their social life had been so dull, and that this was a small request compared to all that he had given up due to her depression.

I repeated my question to Roland. "Can you tell Marcy the feelings you heard from her?" With an impatient edge to his voice, he said, "She thinks it's too much work, but it isn't! And I have rights too! Besides, I will help her when I can." I asked Marcy to briefly restate her feelings; Roland again was unable to hear or articulate them. So I tried to model what that might be like, stating what feelings I heard. Again, he responded with his own feelings and agenda, as well as questioning her assessment of the magnitude of the task.

The session was an eye-opener to me, and I heard many similar conversations between them in later sessions. Marcy could articulate her feelings and his. He was unable to either hear or acknowledge her feelings, and when I stated them, he questioned their validity. I tried several ways of teaching him to listen, hear, and paraphrase her feelings. He never was able to do so.

I found that I was often exhausted after a session with them. Eventually, I felt I was dealing with a depressed woman and a narcissistic man. Roland appeared to be the nice, young, church-going, talented businessman who provided well for his wife and family, yet he was unable to connect emotionally to his wife, unable to empathically hear her feelings. Marcy's depression made it difficult for her to assert herself, or to trust that her feelings and opinions were valuable.

Eventually, I decided that the couple's counseling was going nowhere, Marcy's depression was not improving, and that we needed to return to individual therapy with her. We worked for several more months together, focusing on assertiveness skills and her image of herself as chronically inadequate in every arena of her life. I also encouraged her to join a women's Bible study in her church led by a clergywoman. The conflicts with Roland increased, and her depression lifted. I saw the two developments as clearly related. Marcy terminated therapy, once she was feeling better, and I have often wondered whether and how she has continued to grow.

Female Depression and Male Narcissism

This couple piqued my curiosity about the relationship between depressed women and essentially self-centered men. Is this behind the rash of self-help books for "women who love men who hate them," and "grotesque men unable to love nice women" and "why are there so many hideous men out there?" and "All Single Men: Self-Serving or Gay" and "The Couple of the Nineties: Masochistic Woman, Sadistic Man"? It did seem that I often saw a combination of a depressed woman and a man with limited capacities to give emotionally. And I thought: What is going on?

I developed a theory, based on a longitudinal, or a lifespan, view of depression. Maybe depression preceded the choice of mates. Rather than depression beginning in the context of an inadequate intimate relationship, the problem may well have begun before the relationship and led to the formation of that particular problematic relationship. A vulnerability to depression may have preexisted and led to the choice of men with certain narcissistic qualities. This claim rests on the assumption that affective disorder is the substrate that affects many aspects of a person's life, including her choice of mate.

The narcissistic man is a combination of grandiosity and profound inner brokenness. Because his narcissism includes a deep, unhealed emotional wound, from childhood abuse or neglect, he will display the contradictory qualities of vigorous self-promotion and emotional neediness. He has very limited empathic capacities; limited capacity to see the world, himself, a problem, or anything from another's perspective; and limited ability to imagine what another is feeling. Many if not most of his actions are based on getting his needs met, even if the actions appear to be altruistic. The question then becomes, why are narcissistic men attractive to depressed women?

I can suggest several reasons. (1) We can speculate that it has to do with the self-hatred that accompanies depression. This increases the possibility that a woman will choose a man she perceives as damaged. (2) In addition, at some level a depressed woman may perceive a vague inner inadequacy or weakness that she has yet to name as the illness of affective disorder. For that reason, a man who is as flawed or wounded as she perceives herself to be will appear to offer the promise of a unique kind of intimate connection. She may confuse her illness, an affective disorder, with his damaged self and resulting difficulties with intimate connections. It is critical that women learn to distinguish between a treatable mood disorder and a deeply entrenched personality disorder. On the surface both appear as wounds, yet the mood disorder does not penetrate the deep structures of the personality in the way that a personality disorder does. The recessed and hidden self of depression is not the fragmented or damaged self of personality disorder.

There are other reasons women with affective disorders may choose narcissistic men. (3) Depression also hinders the ability to feel connected to another. To a depressed woman a narcissistic man may not appear to be so because she is hindered in her ability to accurately perceive another's capacity for connection. To some very depressed women, to whom deep connection can feel like simply too much work, it may feel like a relief to not be asked for intimacy. (4) Also, a depressed woman who has very little energy for initiative or creative engagement may also find it a relief to be in a relationship with someone who wishes to be in charge. The depressed woman mistrusts her ability to make decisions and discern a wise course of action. It can be a relief to be with someone who will call the shots when the blankness of self and desire render it difficult to make decisions or take action. (5) The idealization of oneness in a relationship, where the two become one, is attractive to a person whose access to self has been eroded by depression. It seems to baptize the eclipse of their self by saying, "You don't need to emerge from your depression, you don't need to reaccess your self, because your self is now to be found in your mate." (6) Finally, a depressed woman who has little access to a sense of self may feel that she has nothing but the truth of religion to rely on. For the Christian woman, this means giving, sacrificing, self-negating in relationship. The narcissistic man certainly provides a black hole of need for this impulse to give unceasingly.

Sadly, the qualities of narcissistic men that are attractive to women with affective disorders are the very qualities that deepen their depression. So a depressed woman will choose a narcissistic man as a mate, and become all the more depressed. It is critical for caregivers to recognize this unhealthy coupling that is so detrimental to women. A lifespan perspective on depression suggests that we raise the important question of how the illness may have affected the choice of mates.

Depression and Family Systems

In Marcy's case, we can raise the question of the ongoing effect of living with a narcissistic man. Will she continue to be vulnerable to depression? The persistent effects of the family environment are an area that is addressed by family systems thinking that undergirds family therapy. In a discussion of women, relationships, and depression, there must be a consideration of the family, the center of relatedness for most women. In this area, family systems theory and psychotherapy have made important contributions.

When a problem such as depression is seen in systems perspective, it is seen as an adaptive response to that particular family's process. Psychopathology is no longer localized in an individual, whose behavior may in fact be perfectly appropriate to that system. Pathology is identified in the system in which the "problem symptom" arises. To understand depression, then, the family therapist examines the system that produces it in one of the constituent parts. "Thus, rather than assume that a depressed family member has a predisposition to that behavior under stress, the family therapist tries to help the family become aware of how depression in one of its members is an appropriate response to what is happening to them here and now."[9] With this understanding of depression, family therapy of depression consists of changing the processes, rules, and roles that make a depressed member a part of its functioning. In other words, the therapist tries to find ways to change the family's habitual functioning so that depression becomes maladaptive in the particularities of that system.

Like most schools of psychotherapy, family therapy has been subject to feminist critique. Feminists have criticized the following assumptions imbedded in family therapy that belie sexist bias.

> Women are and should be the primary caretakers of children; mothers are the source of problems in those children; the "prototypical clinical family" of enmeshed mother and peripherally involved father is ubiquitous; all families are unique and therefore social patterns are irrelevant; "masculine" characteristics are superior to "feminine" ones.[10]

These assumptions clearly mirror patriarchal, depressogenic elements of the ambient culture, and are therefore problematic for the treatment of depressed women. Rachel Hare-Mustin claims that family systems theory ignores the power differences between family members, assuming that each one has equal access to power.

> Systems approaches, by viewing family members as equal interacting parts in recursive complementarities, tend to ignore differences in power, resources, needs, and interests among family members. Such theories regard the nondifferential treatment of family members as equal treatment, assuming that men and women in the normal family are at the same hierarchical level.[11]

Nevertheless, family therapy has made important contributions to the psychotherapy of depressed women. Systems thinking has brought a new and useful perspective to the powerful influence of family and interpersonal matrices. Most therapists would agree that women's depression cannot be treated apart from the matrix of intimate relationships in which she is imbedded. To address only an individual woman's psychic distress without attending to a depressogenic family system leaves her vulnerable to recurring episodes of depression. The powerful depression-producing conditions would remain intact and continue their eroding effects. Feminist versions of family therapy methods which recognize unequal distributions of power enhance its effectiveness with depressed women.

Relationship as Resource in Pastoral Counseling

We have discussed an orientation toward relationship as a characteristic many women share, though not necessarily intrinsically female. We have also noted that this propensity has been labeled as weakness in traditional streams of psychological thinking. Such an orientation, it has been said, leaves women vulnerable to depression whenever there is a relationship loss or disturbance. Feminist psychologists have pointed out that, far from being a weakness, this relational propensity protects women from depression. A woman's capacity to seek deep connection to others and to give attention to the nurture of these relationships is, in fact, a deterrent to depression, not a contributor to depression.

Relationality in women is also a resource in the psychotherapy of depressed women. Feminists Mary Ballou and Nancy Gabalac have described an approach to counseling that draws on these relational qualities in women. The therapeutic process they present takes relationship, both damaging and healing, very seriously. They present five steps.

1. A movement toward *separation* of the woman from the pervasive negative messages encourages her to tell her own story to the counselor and to other women. As she tells her own story and hears others' stories, a greater sense of the reality of the world around grows, as does her confidence in her ability to know what is real.

2. In the story-telling process, the counselor works for *validation* of the woman's experience and helps her affirm her strengths, which may have been defined as weakness all of her life.

3. *Association* with other women is a crucial part of counseling. Women's groups should be available for women's affiliation and empowerment.

4. *Authorization* is learning to be strong and accountable for oneself. It does not mean falsely independent but rather knowing oneself well enough to have boundaries and still to recognize interdependency.

5. The *negotiation* phase is the testing out, with the ongoing support of counselor and group, of these new behaviors and thoughts in the woman's day-to-day environment.[12]

This therapeutic process can be seen as a choreography of players that includes a woman, her counselor, and a supportive community of women. Therefore, therapy is not confined to the one-to-one relationship between a woman and her therapist. Rather it includes affiliation with a group of women who will affirm the emerging but fragile self. Relationality, the capacity to connect deeply to a supportive community, is integral to therapy described in this way.

Writing a Woman's Life

Most feminist approaches to psychotherapy include space for a woman to freely give voice to her experiences as the beginning of healing. Christie Neuger points to the importance of including a spiritual dimension to the story telling. "Despite her lifelong training that her experience is not valuable or even normative, naming and claiming her story in the presence of one who represents God helps to open up a woman to the powerful presence of the Spirit."[13] Ballou and Gabalac also include in their model the "storytelling process" as a central movement in the empowerment of women. In the last two decades we have heard much about the importance of women "telling their story," and "finding their voice," being "heard into speech."[14] All of these are speaking-hearing metaphors for the process of women coming into their own, understanding themselves in their own terms, speaking the unspeakable, bringing the hidden into light, the shameful into company, discovering "themselves." The speak-hearing metaphor is relational at its core: there is a speaker and a hearer in relationship.

I would like to add another metaphor for the same process of coming into one's own: "writing one's life." I borrow it from Carolyn G. Heilbrun's *Writing a Woman's Life* on the subject of women's biography and autobiography. "There are four ways to write a woman's life: the woman herself may tell it, in what she chooses to call an autobiography; she may tell it in what she chooses to call fiction; a biographer, woman or man, may write the woman's life in what is called a biography; or the woman may write her own life in advance of living it, unconsciously, and without recognizing or naming the process."[15] Heilbrun claims that, until recently, women have lived out of alien narratives, the narratives of family, romance, marriage, motherhood. Heilbrun does not disparage any of these choices for women. But she protests these being the only options for women, at the expense of a place in the public and work realms, and she protests the scripts for these roles being written from a patriarchal perspective. She says that "women have been deprived of the narratives, or the texts, plots, or examples, by which they might assume power over—take control of—their own lives."[16] Heilbrun wishes to lift up the sorts of biographies and autobiographies of women's lives that show the fullness of women's strengths, pains, accomplishments, ambitions, sacrifices in the hope that those of us who read them will have new narratives, plots by which to live our lives, or, rather, by which to write our lives in the living of them.

Adding "writing one's life" to "speaking" metaphors for therapeutic change captures several aspects of the process of the transformation of the self that occurs in psychotherapy. Writing suggests carefully crafting a new work of art. It suggests the painful shaping and reshaping of the new. It suggests rough drafts, false starts, incompleteness, frustration, and writer's block. It also suggests the mystery of imagination and creativity, the experience of giftedness and graciousness of insight and discovery. It suggests drawing on the literary canon for organizing motifs, central images, and recurrent themes. And in the process of appropriating aspects of the canon, the writer disrupts the canon's categories, breaks its bounds, rearranges its forms, genres, plots, typologies, and even what counts as literature. What was originally disparaged as trivial, artless, confused, or overly hyperbolic, emerges as an altogether new reworking of the literary tradition itself. Writing also suggests the materiality of a text, words made permanent and public in ink. Finally, and most important, when Heilbrun speaks of the woman who writes "her own life in advance of living it," the metaphor "writing" captures the notion of forging, creating, shaping a life as a work of art *in the act of* living it. As a woman actively shapes and creates her future, she writes her life.

While writing suggests the lonely author holed up in solitude performing her craft, we can conceive of a woman writing her life in the therapeutic relationship as a shared venture, as a process of writing together new chapters of a woman's life. The therapist is bearer of text from traditional and nontraditional sources, encourages new readings of them, and encourages the creative process of constructing a life-text. The woman and her therapist collaborate, to borrow a term from cognitive therapy literature, in the creative process of writing her life.

Writing captures the fundamentally hermeneutical aspects of psychotherapy, which is often described as the process of remembering the past in a new way, through a more gracious, reconciling lens, and envisioning a future in a more hopeful way. As they are remembered, the events of the past are inevitably sorted, selected, and cast in terms that are condemning, empowering, liberating, enslaving, entrapping, forgiving, or releasing. The prospects for the future are interpreted as offering bounty and possibility, or bleakness, emptiness, despair, and no exit. Just as writing involves hermeneutical choices, so does the therapeutic process. Cognitive therapy can be understood as a fundamentally hermeneutical process: changing the interpretive schemes from depressogenic to healthy ones.

In the hermeneutical, constructive process that is psychotherapeutic change, biblical images offer helpful interpretive lenses through which to remember the past and shape the future. If the client is in the process of writing a life, creating a new text, the therapist can be a bearer of the old text from the biblical canon. The therapist can offer biblical images that bring hints of their literary context, whether it be a narrative, psalmic, Gospel, parable, epistolary, or any other biblical genre. For example, wilderness suggests pillars of cloud and fire, manna, promised land, milk and honey. In shepherd one hears the hints of still waters, green pastures, and a cup that overflows. In the cross, there are multiple layers of echo, such as anguish and redemption, tragedy and resurrection, evil and love, defeat and vindication, victim and victor.[17] To say exile is also to say Jerusalem, home, temple. To say mustard seed is also to say kingdom of God. To say Egypt is to say Red Sea. To say Mount Sinai is to say covenant and golden calf. Saying principalities and powers echoes the affirmation that nothing can separate us from the love of God in Jesus Christ. To consider yourself weary and heavy laden is to hear echoes of the one who invites you to come unto him and who offers rest.

In this hermeneutical process the pastor can move away from presenting scripture as the truth to which the parishioner submits or asserting the authority to give the definitive interpretation. The pastor will be less likely to limit or control the image to meet their predetermined end. Good counseling depends on suggestion, understatement, allowing the client to be the writer, the author, the authority, not the pastor.

The biblical images are heard in a social context. In speaking of biblical texts and images, the pastoral counselor evokes connections to other communities, other relational networks. In hearing words of scripture, the client will also hear echoes of the community that first taught them the Bible. The proverbial "mother's knee," the Sunday school teacher, the saints of the church from whom we first learned the meaning of forgiveness, hope, love, faith, rebirth, and so forth, will all be heard as echoes of biblical images. And the client will hear echoes of the present community, its voices, resonances, tones, chords, meanings, in these images. In addition to the childhood community and the current community, there is the context of the therapeutic relationship. The trustworthiness of the pastoral counselor is crucial. The imprint of the care and healing experienced in the therapeutic setting will inevitably echo in the biblical image. The bearer of the biblical text, in other words, is also important in discerning the echoes.

Secular psychotherapy has discovered the power of working with imagery. Workshops on "guided imagery" show how to connect with deep, inner images and begin to transform them. This has been experienced by many as a powerful and healing exercise. However, popular uses of imagery in working with the inner landscape has leaned toward a "smorgasbord" approach to images that borrows from many discourses: Kahlil Gibran, astrology, Myers-Briggs, New Age, I Ching, Jungian archetypes, twelve-step literature, and so forth. While any of these sources might offer powerful, creative, novel images to serve as a hermeneutic for the writing of one's life in psychotherapy, they tend to be estranged from historical, communal, and cultural context. The pastoral psychotherapist who draws on biblical imagery brings echoes of canonical context, historical community, memory, and a host of literary, social, and liturgical contexts. The biblical image is tied to myriad contextual anchors.

Therapeutic change as "writing a life" suggests the importance of relationship with the therapist as temporary coauthor or the creative consultant. It also suggests a reading community, the ones who will read the text and be shaped by it, come into relationship with it, even construct the text in the reading of it.[18] It also suggests the connection to the ancient biblical community that gave rise to the scriptural texts, the church community that first proclaimed it in childhood, and the church community that continues to give it witness in the present. "Writing one's life" as a metaphor adds to "telling one's story" as an important way of conceiving the relational process that is therapeutic change.

Theological Perspective

Several biblical texts came to mind as I pondered Marcy's problematic personal theology. "Not what I want, but what you want" (Mark 14:36). "Here am I, the servant of the Lord; let it be with me according to your word" (Luke 1:38). "The fruit of the Spirit is . . . self-control" (Gal. 5:22–23). She was not haunted by fears of hell and eternal condemnation, nor was she plagued by guilt and a deep sense of her own sinfulness. Rather she felt chronically inadequate, had a low-grade dissatisfaction with her spiritual life, and thought that it was her own fault. Clearly, her piety consisted of self-emptying, self-eviscerating, in order to hear and do the will of God.

I thought of another scriptural text for her, one that could serve as a helpful hermeneutic for her as she goes about the process of telling her story or writing her life. I wondered if the story of the woman cured of the flow of blood might be a model for her (Mark 5:25–34). The woman's malady had rendered her ritually unclean for twelve years, because anyone she touched would become unclean as well. Therefore, she was cut off from human warmth, touch, and community for twelve years. She heard reports of the healer Jesus coming to town, so she joined the thronging crowds around him. She reached out, touched his garment, and immediately was healed. She reached out over the crowds, over centuries of the oppression of women, over religious law that called her unclean, over the years of illness and ostracism, and touched Jesus. Immediately, she was healed of her disease and restored to human community.

When Jesus asked who touched him, she fell down before him and "told him the whole truth." What did she say to Jesus? What is it to tell Jesus the whole truth of yourself? Did she speak of her loneliness, pains, rages, shame?

We are accustomed to thinking of this woman as pale and sickly, as meekly, apologetically, pathetically reaching for Jesus. I would like to suggest a different picture. I suggest she was a woman who had had it, who was sick and tired of the loneliness, mess, and ostracism. So in an act of desperation, or rage, or rebellion, she reached out for Jesus. And Jesus told her that her faith made her well. If we were to define faith based only on this story, we would have to say it was her boldness.[19] Her faith was her willingness to break through the religious and cultural expectations of her as an unclean woman and to touch the popular healer Jesus. This was a courageous, countercultural act, a defiant reaching for her health and wholeness. In truth, we do not know the state of her heart. We only know what she did; she boldly risked reaching for Jesus, and it was that which made her well.

I wonder if Marcy will ever be able to boldly reach for her health and healing. I wonder if Jesus can ever be for her the one to whom she tells the whole truth of her life. I wonder if she can see this Bible woman's bold act as faith, recognizing that faith can be the defiant reach for Jesus on your own behalf, instead of "getting out of the way" in order to know and do God's will.

In so many ways, traditional Christian theology encourages a style of relationship where women's selves are sacrificed to the other. Whether that other is children, God, or husband, the woman is to set aside her well-being, opinions, and feelings and, in a word, to "get out of the way." It is important for the caregiver to explore a depressed woman's image of the good relationship, and what qualities of a person she believes are required. The pastoral caregiver can offer scriptural and traditional resources for a style of relationship that involves self-care, self-love, and the nurture of the self.

Even as the chapter on "self" was incomplete without a discussion of relationships, so is this chapter inadequate without a discussion of self. What I would wish most for Marcy, and for all depressed women, is an "encounter with the holy mystery of their own selves as blessed," in the words of Elizabeth Johnson.[20] "[K]nown in the surge of self-affirmation," she says, is a "new experience of God as beneficent toward the female and an ally of women's flourishing."[21] I would want Marcy and all depressed women to understand conversion, or coming into deeper relationship with God, "not as giving up the self but as tapping into the power of oneself [which] simultaneously releases understanding of divine power, not as dominating power-over but as the passionate ability to empower oneself and others."[22]

Chapter Six

Women's Bodies

The Female Body has many uses. It's been used as a door knocker, a bottle opener, as a clock with a ticking belly, as something to hold up lampshades, as a nutcracker, just squeeze the brass legs together and out comes your nut. It bears torches, lifts victorious wreaths, grows copperwings, and raises aloft a ring of neon stars; whole buildings rest on its marble heads.

It sells cars, beer, shaving lotion, cigarettes, hard liquor; it sells diet plans and diamonds, and desire in tiny crystal bottles. Is this the face that launched a thousand products? You bet it is but don't get any funny big ideas, honey, that smile is a dime a dozen.

—*Margaret Atwood*[1]

Depression is an event of the body. It involves a physiological change in brain chemistry and neurological processes. Depression is a matter of various neurotransmitters, the functioning of nerve receptor sites, the workings of complex biochemical and nervous interactions. The body is also implicated in its symptoms—many of the symptoms are physical: energy level, appetite, sleep, sex drive. For some, the genesis of depression is a matter of disjointed circadian rhythms, governed by that delicate inner clock that coordinates the eating and sleeping activities of the body with the changing levels of sunlight. Not only do the symptoms and genesis of depression include the body, but the treatment of depression includes the body in the form of antidepressant medication. Some physiological interventions include bright light therapy for those who have seasonal depressions. Other treatments include deliberate changes in sleep patterns, while still others adjust hormone levels in the body. In short, the body is thoroughly involved in depression. Any discussion of depression must include a consideration of the body.

For women, the body is implicated even further, and several themes can be identified. First, cultural attitudes toward women's bodies affect our vulnerability to depression: patriarchal culture tends to view women's bodies as commodity, with a constricted image of beauty as the currency. This feature of patriarchy has been immeasurably destructive to women in many ways, including contributing to the prevalence of depression among women. Second, depression lends itself to distorted images of the self, and often this takes the form of a distorted body image, especially in a misogynist culture. Culture and depression form an unholy union to further women's hatred of their body-selves. Third, women's bodies are subject to male control through violence and the threat of violence, such as sexual abuse, rape, or battering. This vulnerability contributes not only to a woman's belief that she is powerless, but also in fact to diminishing her power. A sense of powerlessness, it has been established, is a central hallmark of depression. Fourth, women's capacity to bear children contributes to the personal and social meanings of the female body. These meanings interact with the very real physiological changes in a woman's body during menstruation, pregnancy, and menopause.

Therefore, it is critical that female embodiment be taken seriously in the pastoral counseling of depressed women. This chapter begins with these themes and psychotherapeutic responses to them.

It is significant that at no point in the writing of this book have I so felt my limitations as an author. It is at the point of bodies that the diversity of women is highlighted. Women's bodies differ by skin color, hair texture, shape of eye and nose and mouth; our bodies differ by youth or age, by ability or disability, by sexual orientation as lesbian, straight, or bisexual. Embodiment captures a very deep part of what connects and divides us as women. It is my hope that this chapter will deal with issues that connect us as women in a patriarchal world. Yet I am deeply aware of how embodiment shapes knowledge and creativity, and that my perspective is skewed by the particular form my body takes, and the privilege or prejudice that it implies. As a white, heterosexual, middle class, middle-aged citizen of the United States, I have both insight and blindness. That fact will be most apparent in this chapter.

Women's Bodies as Commodity

I think about my body too much. In the morning, as I lie in bed deciding what to wear, I try to construct an outfit that will reconstruct my body, or at least camouflage it, or play tricks with illusions built with scarves, belts, necklines, print lines, hemlines. Do I want to appear professional and businesslike, or whimsical, or countercultural? While this may seem

*like a luxury, to have such a glorious array of options, it feels like a bur-
den this morning. I would really rather go to work looking unnoticeably
regular, and not have to decide on what I want to portray, because the one
option I don't have is not having an image, the option of making no statement.*

*Putting on my makeup, I inspect the lines in my face. Are they ad-
vancing? And what about those gray hairs? Has the time finally come to
color my hair? I reconsider the question for the millionth time as I gaze in
the mirror.*

*There are great things at stake in these body decisions. See, I have lodged
in my consciousness two very important axioms: if I am to find love, I must
be thin and pretty; if I am to reach professional goals, I must be thin and
pretty. When contemplating my life, and my future, and thinking how to go
where I want to go, how to build the life that I want, it always points to the
answer, "I must lose weight." I will not find a mate unless I am thinner, I
will not be perceived as competent unless I am thinner. For me, thin =
power. And now, as I age, I feel a new tyranny emerging, the tyranny of
youth. Soon, I'm sure a new axiom will emerge: young = power.*

*As I drive to work in my car without air conditioning, I keep the win-
dows rolled up to protect my carefully sprayed hair. It is a difficult bal-
ancing act, because excessive sweat can also ruin one's makeup.*

*The workday begins with a meeting. I am acutely aware of how I am sit-
ting. I want to appear strong and competent. Do I do the feminine thing and
try to occupy as little space as possible, or do I do the all-business pose, with
hands and feet planted firmly? The meeting is over, time for lunch. Again,
the tyranny of weight: every mouthful is connected to my body-self and, as
you recall, connected to my sense of personal and professional goals. Such
noisy voices to have in one's consciousness when just trying to have a little lunch! Such high stakes!*

The above account of a single day captures the tyranny of occupying a female body in a culture where "woman as body" is a dominant paradigm.[2] The
defining power attached to women's bodies, in combination with constricted
beauty standards, gives rise to women's overwhelming tendency to give negative assessment to their bodies. This lethal combination renders a woman's
body image a crucial area of therapeutic exploration with depressed women.

In our culture, women's bodies are seen as a source of power: the measure of her beauty is the measure of her power. The most exaggerated form
of this is prostitution. To sell—or perhaps rent is more accurate—your
body in exchange for cash, is a way of gaining access to the power to pay
the bills. Bikini-clad models at a car show play a similar role. All adolescent
girls learn that the pretty girls are more powerful, in the ways that count at

that age, than the not-so-pretty girls: cheerleading and boys and often the favorable gaze of teachers, especially if their attractiveness is backed by family status. Also, the beautiful women tend to be chosen by the men with access to power: powerful men want to "purchase" wives whose power is measured in the currency of beauty. Therefore, women considered beautiful will have access to social and economic power through their husbands.

Beauty is the currency for women, money and status is the currency for men. Beauty is a unit of exchange, the currency that gains women access to such social goods as position and money. However, the cost is high. When women appropriate the cultural norm of body as commodity, the cost is manifold, including depression. First of all, viewing body as commodity is hardly a form of self-love. In the final analysis, according to Miriam Greenspan,

> If a woman's power is centered in her body, so ultimately, is her power-lessness. Because in patriarchal society a woman's body does not belong to her—it is appropriated by and for men. It is defined as an object for men's use. Whether in providing heirs or sexual service for men, the power of a woman's body is ultimately subservient to male needs and interests.[3]

Second, women's bodies are only useful commodities for a brief span of years. Aging female bodies lose their rate of exchange, and every woman knows this. Third, and perhaps most damaging, when a beautiful body is the only access to power, or when women are taught that this is the only access to power, women do not develop or tap other kinds of power, such as the power of friendship, the power of skill, the power to nurture, and the power of knowledge. Power as capacity and power as relationship are underdeveloped.[4] Furthermore, there is a narrow range of physical features that qualify as beautiful. This means that most women fall far short of the beauty standards of the dominant culture and women judge themselves as unattractive. This is a very effective way of convincing women that they have little power at their disposal: tell them that beauty is power, then create impossible beauty standards. Women quickly get the message: you are powerless.

Women of color are especially victimized by narrow, European standards of beauty. One woman of color described being "exiled from what is considered 'normal,' white-right."[5] Cheryl Townsend Gilkes states, "Black women are still peculiarly victimized by the cult of beauty and the culture of sexual exploitation, abuse, and violence it masks."[6] She speaks of the complexity of attitudes toward African American women's bodies in a racist, sexist society. She describes the compounded oppression of both racism and sexism, greater than simply additive effects of each, that results in cultural stereotypes of the promiscuous, seductive Jezebel, and its opposite in the asexual, maternal Mammy. She also describes an ambivalence within the African American community, where the thin, light-skinned woman with Euro-American features is assigned a different role than the larger, dark-skinned, full-featured woman.

Black women's bodies are commodified not only in the currency of beauty, but in the currency of labor. Patricia Hill Collins names other oppressive images of African American women and how they are implicated into the political economy. She names the mammy as the domestic worker in a white household, "an asexual woman, a surrogate mother in blackface devoted to the development of a white family."[7] We can understand her body implicated not only as it is not given to sexual pleasure, but as it is devoted to the bodily care and sustenance of the white family in her domestic work. The matriarch is the maternal image of the black woman in the black home, and it is the image of the failed mother. Her work outside her home renders her an inadequate mother; her aggressiveness emasculates husband or lover.[8]

The welfare mother is yet another image Collins defines. According to the stereotype, this woman is lazy, a "breeder woman," and unwed.[9] In other words, she is a woman whose body is not controlled in patriarchal marriage, and the result is "rampant" rates of childbirth and an unproductive, unemployed unit of labor. Finally, Collins names Jezebel as a cultural image of black women. This is the sexually aggressive woman, and it is the image behind the other three. Collins claims that what is behind all the images is an attempt to control black women's sexuality and fertility for the purposes of controlling their roles in the political economy.[10] Again, we can see the interconnection between female embodiment and patriarchal efforts to commodify them.

Women of color face particular oppressions not experienced by those marked "white" in a racist culture, and white women are usually oblivious to the ways we benefit from racial identity in a culture that privileges whiteness. Until we do, we will be divided as women and disabled in the struggle against forces that dehumanize us all.

Depression's Distortions and Culture's Lies

The problem of "woman's body as commodity" is magnified for the depressed woman. Depression, for men and women, brings with it a negative view of the body. Sylvia Plath, in her journals, recorded this notion of her body:

> I go plodding on, afraid the blank hell in back of my eyes will break through, spewing forth like dark pestilence, afraid that the disease which eats away the pith of my body with merciless impersonality will break forth in obvious sores and warts, screaming "Traitor, sinner, imposter."[11]

When the depressed person is a woman, the negative view of one's body is reinforced by impossible beauty standards. If a non-depressed woman judges herself physically inadequate, a depressed woman has even more distorted and exaggerated notions of her failure to live up to the cultural standards of beauty.

Therefore, *psychotherapeutically*, the task is, first, to unmask the ways that culture has taught us to use our bodies as commodities in exchange for social goods—to reveal the self-defeating nature of that kind of power—and, second, to develop other forms of power.

The pastoral counselor begins by helping the woman to describe herself physically. This will almost certainly be a distorted view. For example, at this particular time in history, American culture values thin women. So, when depressed, a normal-sized woman will describe herself as fat, a slightly overweight woman will describe herself as hideously obese, a significantly obese woman will believe herself unworthy of life itself. The pastor or therapist can then begin to gently point out the exaggerations in these perceptions. To the normal-sized woman, "What is a *healthy* weight for you?" "Where exactly are you fat?" "Who are you supposed to look like?, and who said so?" "Exactly who established that you are fat?" Often, in the course of these questions, it emerges that it is unrealistic cultural standards that are at fault, and not one's own body. The pastoral caregiver can establish that, for a woman, one's weight is not the problem, nor is it a reason to hate oneself. Again, the problem is in the culture, in the beauty as commodity notion, and not in her value as a human being. This is an example of a therapist working with one particular cultural pressure on women, especially young women, the pressure to be thin. Other pressures abound: large breasts, long legs, small waist, flawless skin, light skin if you are dark, tan skin if you are light.

Another therapeutic approach is to develop other positive body images, allowing the negative images to temporarily remain. Author Pam Houston wrote about her body experiences. Her intriguing style takes the reader back and forth between captivity to patriarchal hatred of women's bodies and descriptions of exhilaration with her body. First,

> When I was younger, I used to believe that if I were really thin I would be happy, and there is a part of me that still believes it's true. For a good part of my life I would have quite literally given anything to be thin . . . a finger, three toes, the sight in one eye. Now I find it only mildly surprising that for the majority of my lifetime I would have traded being ugly, deformed, and thin for being pretty, whole, and fat.[12]

And then, immediately after, she describes approaching a section of whitewater as she steers a raft, having just witnessed a raft steered by her husband, "the strongest human being I know," unsuccessfully negotiate a difficult passage, and in the process, lose passengers in the water and crack into a wall of stone.[13] She tells of her approach to the difficult passage.

> Every synapse in my brain and every muscle in my body is focused on pulling away from that [stone] wall. My feet, my thighs, my stomach, my back, my arms, my hands all work together, in a movement that is, I think, very like a wave, to bring the oars upstream against the rushing water. The wall gets closer and closer, and just when I think I am doing no good at all I feel the boat responding, moving backward against the current that's been driving it toward the rock. The nose of the boat barely kisses the wall and one more stroke pulls us safely away.
> "Damn," says one of the Texans. "Hot damn."
> We go to work rescuing the other boat's passengers.[14]

We can be instructed by this example. Self-loathing body statements cannot be eradicated immediately; they linger, and sometimes for a lifetime. But they can be made to fade out, and to lose power, by the addition of other body images that emerge from experiences of the body as powerful, skilled, and a source of exhilaration. Depressed women can be encouraged to experience their body in many ways, not just as a commodity. Our bodies can be experienced as strong in rafting and agile in rock climbing. We can know our bodies as sources of sensual pleasure via massage and gentle touch, or feeling the warm sun or a cool breeze. We can love our bodies for the pleasures they bring in lovemaking. We can experience our bodies as developing skill at tennis or golf or racquetball. We can know the amazement of pointing our skis downhill, risking injury, for the sake of amazing speed. We can know that perseverance-beyond-perseverance of long distance running, passing "the wall" and moving into a rhythm of footfall, breath, and whatever song keeps the beats in the mind. Dance, whether the strenuous demands of ballet or the socially enjoyable international folk dancing, or the sensual sway to a saxophone, or the creations of rhythms of feet and hands, these body experiences make one revel in embodiedness, not hate one's body. These experiences move one away from a focus on body as commodity. In addition, a good aerobic workout can alter the brain chemistry in a way that is very effective in lifting mood.

There are other experiences of the body that do not require physical strength and agility. For women who are physically challenged, or women whose age limits their sheer strength, aerobic activities other than running or walking or dancing may be explored. Apart from aerobic body experience there is also the experience of the body in the exercise of creativity in pottery making, cabinet building, furniture refinishing, and in the largely unrecognized "women's" arts of knitting, crocheting, quilting, sewing, and even cooking that involve dexterity and ingenuity. The hands and their power to create are remarkable. The experience of body also includes the skill of the musician. Any guitarist's calluses are a reminder of how physical that art is. Players of wind and brass instruments know how important breath discipline is. Singers of the blues, singers of the opera, are well aware of how much the body is involved in the creation of musical sound. Music makers know the importance of the body as a source of art and beauty. Strenuous exercise is certainly not off-limits for many disabled or aging women, but for those who are excluded from a rigorous workout, other body experiences are possible.

Our clients can be encouraged to name these skills as experiences of their bodies, or, if they are not engaged in any of these activities, they can be encouraged to expand their repertoire of body experiences. A woman who learns to think of the many alternative ways of thinking of her body, its skill, sources of pleasure, adventure, and exhilaration can develop a new love and appreciation for her body. As a note to the pastoral counselor, it is not required that the old, dysfunctional ways of viewing body-self be purged immediately. Newer ones can be introduced alongside them.

Once a woman has begun to deal with the hegemonic negative body-self images, she can begin to reexamine the ambient culture. It is not enough to deal at an individual psychological level with these images. A woman must take a proactive stance toward the oppressive cultural myths about women's bodies. She must be given the choice of how to respond to this culture. This can take several forms.

1. Help her to recognize that, though advertisers would have you think otherwise, there really is a broad range of ideal types. The Marilyn Monroe type, the thin Vogue model type, and the girl-next-door type represent a sampling of ideal types that are quite different from each other. However much you resist these types, and find them oppressive, it is still worth noting that there is no agreement on a single type of female beauty.

2. Point out that American culture, while there is a dominant culture, nevertheless embraces a wide variety of subcultures. Ethnic subcultures expand the range of female beauty: hair, skin, body proportions; these vary from group to group. There are also athletic subcultures, lesbian subcultures, artistic subcultures, intellectual subcultures, and alternative political subcultures that each carry variations on what is attractive. The point is not to find a subculture where everyone considers your particular type attractive. The point is that there is no monolithic consensus out there about what is physically attractive. This gives a woman the sense that she is not imprisoned for a lifetime in a body considered hideous by all.

3. Explore just how important the standard type is, how worthwhile it is to conform to it. She may choose to ignore, or at least depart from, the dominant standard. This gives a woman a sense that she has options, that she can choose how to live in the world as it is. It is empowering to know that a countercultural option is possible. It develops her sense of agency, power over the dominant beauty images.

4. Relativize the importance of physical appearance. There are many aspects that render a person attractive! We are all taught this: "it is inner beauty that counts," "but you have such a wonderful personality," "who cares what everybody else thinks, anyway," "just be neat and clean and smile nice." But the power of the cultural standards of beauty to determine self-image usually overrides. I speak of relativizing the importance of physical appearance because to say it has no importance ignores two facts. First, in our culture women will be judged by physical appearance, and a woman needs to be clear about the misogyny out there. Second, a physical element in human relating is not to be shunned or eradicated. Physical attraction is an important part of communication, and a healthy one. To attempt to eliminate it is neither possible nor desirable. Finding someone physically appealing, liking the way someone looks, is a pleasurable way of experiencing another person. The problem arises when there are misogynist, unrealistic, rigid, narrow definitions of what is considered attractive.

Cognitive Therapy and Cultural Images of Women's Bodies

Cognitive therapy offers ways of challenging dominant cultural assumptions about women's bodies. The counselor can inquire about automatic thoughts regarding body. Are there automatic thoughts that belie an appropriation of cultural standards against which any woman of flesh and blood would be found wanting? If so, the automatic thought record can be used to introduce alternative views. For example, Sally, lonely and mildly depressed, strolls through the produce section of a grocery store, and a man who appears to be a nice person asks her how to buy a watermelon. She feels anxiety and then despair in the course of the brief conversation. The counselor asks, "What was going through your mind as you spoke to him?" "My first thought was, I look awful, no makeup, and these shorts make me look so bulgy. In fact, he probably asked me about watermelons because he thinks I look like one."

"Is it possible he was trying to strike up a conversation?"

"No way. Not when I was looking like that."

"Could he have thought you looked natural and easy to talk to?"

"Well, he might have, but that wouldn't be a reason to want to have a friendly conversation with me."

"OK, let me see what the rules are here: one, there exists a standard of beauty, and that is the Vogue standard. Two, all men subscribe to that notion. Three, the only thing attractive about a woman is how she measures up to that standard. Am I right here?"

"Well . . ."

By articulating some of the assumptions underlying the automatic thoughts women often reveal them to be exaggerated, rigid, and oversimplified. This begins to introduce some cracks in the patriarchal assumptions behind many women with a self-loathing body image.

When women become clear about the sources of their negative body images, that they are rooted in distorted, inhuman expectations of women, this is the first step toward freedom from their tyranny. What is tragic about depression is that the illness takes up where the culture lets off: if there is only a narrow range of options for being attractive, and if the culture places a high premium on attractiveness in women, then depression exaggerates this negativity and narrowness even further. What the culture begins, the illness furthers. Therefore many depressed women have sadly distorted images of how they look, their level of physical attractiveness, and their appearance.

There are at least three levels of distortion. Not only is the self-image distorted: "My nose is enormous." But also the gravity of the consequences are distorted as well: "I will never, ever be loved because of my enormous nose." In addition, the standards become more rigid and more narrow. "There is only one kind of acceptable nose in the world, and this is an unwavering, universally held standard." The cognitive model helps us to understand these distortions and offers ways to begin to challenge them.

Counselors can listen carefully for all these assumptions—the distorted self-image, the extreme consequences, the rigid and narrow standard. Using cognitive therapy, they can begin to question these distortions, extremes, and rigidities. "No one will ever love you, ever?" "There is only one acceptable nose in the world?" "No one with your particular nose shape has ever been loved?" These sometimes humorous questions about the validity of underlying assumptions function to erode dysfunctional body images.

Physical Vulnerability

By the end of the day the combination of sore back and feet, waist squeezed all day, the horrid panty hose, I am glad to go home.

I relax, have a little dinner, watch the news, and decide to go for a quick run. Again, do I wear that spandex running top that will keep me cool and comfortable, or do I consider that stretch of isolated road I have to cover? I choose cool, but I pay the price. It is beginning to get dark, and my run is littered with images of a crazy man leaping out of the woods and grabbing me, or a gang of teenage boys driving up with radio blaring and throwing me in the car, or who knows what other possibilities I face in the gathering darkness as I plod along.

In the quote above, the woman noted the fear of going out for a run at twilight. Her run was plagued by disturbing fears of being attacked. Violence against women is a form of social control. The fear of rape controls many aspects of a woman's life. Where to live, working hours, recreational options—all of these require a consideration of physical safety to an extent unimagined by most men. I remember noticing my brothers had traveled alone both domestically and internationally a great deal more than I. Upon reflection, I realized that it was my sense of physical vulnerability that had inhibited my travel. As college students my brothers had a sort of Grand Tour experience, in the United States and abroad, while I did not. Certainly I was as accustomed to travel as they, and I had the desire and love of adventure that they had; the mechanics and skills and savvy of long distance travel were familiar to me. It was solely the sense, and the accurate sense, that I would have been more physically vulnerable than they were that inhibited my travel. While this is not a serious form of inhibition—being deprived of tourist opportunities can hardly be viewed as tragic—this is an example of the disparity in options for women and men wrought by the threat of violence. The social control takes a much more serious turn than being deprived of tourist opportunities.

Many woman feel the day-to-day controlling fear of being battered by husbands or boyfriends. The U.S. Department of Justice tells us a woman is beaten every 15 seconds.[15] The FBI reports that domestic violence is the leading cause of injury to women between the ages of 15 and 44 in the United States, more than car accidents, muggings, and rapes combined.[16] Even leaving a violent marriage will not necessarily protect a woman. In fact, 75 percent of emergency room visits by women who are victims of domestic violence occur after a woman has left her batterer; 75 percent of calls to law enforcement agencies occur after a woman has left her batterer.[17] Pastors and therapists will hear women report that they are literally afraid for their lives. If not in immediate danger, many women are controlled by the unpredictability of male rage and violence. Efforts to placate and to please a man prone to battering are often a woman's attempts to protect her physical integrity.

Cognitive Therapy and Physical Vulnerability

Therapeutically, it is important to remind a woman of the choices and control that she does have. The college-age woman can choose to travel with others. The single woman can live in a downtown apartment on a well-lit corner. The runner can run with someone else or in daylight hours. If a woman believes she is less powerful than she in fact is, she may stay in situations that reinforce her sense of powerlessness. And she may deny herself therapeutic activities, everything from exercise to running or a downtown concert, for fear of her safety.

The battered woman can be urged to seek a safer living environment, notify the police, get court-ordered protection, and so forth. In psychotherapy, the battered woman scarred by learned helplessness can be empowered to name her inner resources of courage, rebellion, ingenuity, and self-love. She can articulate any external resources in the form of sympathetic family, friends, church, or shelters. These choices expand a woman's sense of her power and agency, and combat feelings of defeat and helplessness.

Some may debate the extent of a battered woman's power, arguing that she is, in fact, powerless, and no amount of psychological tinkering or cognitive restructuring will correct the fact of her powerlessness before her batterer. I would agree, that in the phase of "acute battering," as Lenore Walker has described the overtly violent phase of the cycle of violence, a woman is close to utter powerlessness.[18] However, I do not believe life with battering ever eliminates all traces of a woman's power. She will have some resources somewhere, even if the distortions of depression have blinded her to their existence. The double-edged nature of violence against women is that the very real diminishment of a woman's power is joined by the distortions of depression, which hinders a woman from claiming what remaining power she may very well have. A depressed woman is all too ready to give up, to believe she is utterly helpless, utterly without resource or option. She can construe her life options so narrowly that she believes she is more powerless than she in fact is. The caregiver can hear her story, believe her, enable her to begin to see her options, both short-term and long-term, and help her to seek a life where she is safe from violence.

At this point, behavioral activities may be therapeutic. A woman who claims to be unable to exercise can be urged to research all the options, the safe, unthreatening options. A battered woman can be urged to explore alternative living arrangements, with friends or family or at a shelter, or to get a court order to keep a violent man away. "Homework" assignments to make phone calls, ask friends, read the newspaper, or visit a women's shelter, can expand a woman's sense of what viable, safe options are for her. The purpose of this therapeutic strategy is not to paint a rosy picture of the world. Clearly, even with all these steps taken, many women continue to be at risk, or even greater risk, having left a batterer. These efforts to help a woman claim her power are not risk-free. Rather than painting a falsely optimistic picture, cognitive therapy attempts to address the distortions in perception of the world. It is the globalizing tendency among the depressed that must be addressed, the tendency to distort a realistic assessment of women's need for caution in certain circumstances, making it applicable to all situations, and thereby unnecessarily restricting one's life options. The pastor's role is to help a parishioner to see where there may be distortions and to correct them, thereby expanding a woman's options.

Women's Bodies and Reproduction

A common assumption regarding depression in women is that somehow our "female hormones" are involved. The assumption goes like this: There is something having to do with that mysterious realm of menstruation, pregnancy, menopause, and so forth, that makes women depressed more often than men. The problem with this view is that it suggests that women, by virtue of our capacity for bearing children, are somehow born with a greater vulnerability to depression than men.

It would be body-denying to suggest that women's childbearing capacity is irrelevant to a discussion of depression. After all, depression is a biological event, and reproductive capacities are imbedded in our bodies. Yet it must be stressed that depression is a result of the interaction of biology, individual personality, relationships, and social location. The genesis of depression involves multiple interacting factors. Biology—and the reproductive aspects of our bodies—cannot be isolated as the primary cause of high rates of depression in women.

Menopause provides a good example of interacting factors. The biological event that is menopause is also an event in an individual woman's sense of herself and her creative capacities, as well as having social meaning and status implications. Menopause is not only a matter of fluctuating hormones, it also has deep social meanings and may have significant personal meanings as well. It appears that menopause itself does not hormonally trigger depression. However, women who were already depressed before the onset of menopause may experience deeper distress with its beginning. Among women in their forties and fifties, social factors such as teenage children, responsibility for elderly parents, or a husband who is ill are more closely correlated with depression than endocrinological changes.[19]

The research on depression and women's reproduction capacities shows interesting facts. While "premenstrual syndrome" is a trying time for many women, it is not synonymous with depression. Mood changes linked to the menstrual cycle produce many symptoms common to depression, yet at a less severe level. These mood changes cannot be called a full-blown episode of depression.[20] Pregnancy itself is not associated with mood disorders, yet 50 to 80 percent of women experience some sort of mild postpartum affective disturbance that begins three or four days after childbirth and lasts from one to fourteen days. A smaller proportion of women experience a more severe depression that can begin six weeks to four months after childbirth and may last six to twelve months. Again, psychological factors, such as the meaning of pregnancy and birth, and social factors, such as the level of support and marital adjustment, interact with these hormonal changes in women.[21] Women who would like to become pregnant but are unable to because of infertility problems suffer higher rates of depression.[22] In cases of terminated pregnancy, statistics show that abortion poses no more risk for depression than any other significant life event, though again, it depends on the meaning abortion has and the support a woman has in a particular social context.[23] One report notes that positive psychological effects of abortion have not been fully assessed, though one study "found that after an abortion women reported feeling more self-directed and instrumental, reflecting a personality change in the women's sense of autonomy and efficacy."[24]

It is hard to underestimate the importance of dealing with the body when working psychotherapeutically with depressed women. Depression is an event of the body. Many cultural attitudes about women contribute to the high incidence of depression among women, including cultural attitudes specifically about women's bodies. Depression lends itself to distorted images of the self, and often this takes the form of a distorted body image. Women's bodies are a source of vulnerability and male control, which contributes to a woman's sense of powerlessness.

In these four very significant ways, it becomes clear that it is crucial to attend to the body when working with depressed women.

Medication, Cognitive Therapy, and Women

For many who have suffered from depression, anti-depressant medication has made the difference between a grim life with bouts of despair and interpersonal and vocational difficulties, and a life of hopeful expectancy with rewarding relationships and work. Yet many who are depressed are very resistant to suggestions that medication might be useful. The resistance is often based on the belief that "medication means I must be crazy." Other fears are that medication is addictive, brings euphoric highs, or changes the basic personality. Such fears can be addressed by the pastoral caregiver. It is critical that the caregiver be aware of competent psychiatrists or family practice physicians who are able to prescribe and monitor medications skillfully.

The decision to refer to a psychiatrist for medication has been challenged from the perspective of both cognitive therapy and feminism. Some practitioners of cognitive therapy argue that cognitive therapy is sufficient to deal with depression, and that anti-depressant medication is unnecessary. Yet Aaron Beck gives clear criteria for when cognitive therapy is sufficient, and when it is not enough, and medication is required (Beck, et al., 366–68). Therefore, from the perspective of Aaron Beck, anti-depressants are consistent with quality treatment of depression, though not in every case.

From a feminist perspective, the use of medication has been criticized as a form of buying into a medical model of mental health and treatment. This model, the critics say, often results in the insensitive administration of medication by the "expert" without the careful, empathic attention to an individual situation. Feminist pastoral theologian Christie Neuger adds, "Theorists who work from a women's perspective are, on the whole, very cautious about biological approaches as the history of mental health reveals a tendency to overmedicate women as a response to their 'illnesses' or distress."[25]

While these feminist cautions are certainly important ones, it is my perspective that denying the importance of the biological perspective, and a biological treatment, is a form of body denial. It assumes that the mind-body connection is only one way: we attend to the maladies of our mind-body selves, such as depression, only through the mind, psyche, or spirit. This ignores the possibility that the body is a point of intervention as well, that medication, as well as other physiological interventions such as vigorous exercise, can also be healing for the mind-body self. One of the central points of this book is the importance of the consideration of women's bodies in understanding depression. This attention to embodiment is extended to the intricacies of neurochemistry and which interventions will support healing from the physiological state called depression. Of course it would be irresponsible to think that medication alone is enough for most women, though in some cases it is. Clearly the supportive presence of a caring therapist is not only critical to human healing, but is necessary for the behavioral, cognitive, interpersonal changes that are involved in protecting a woman from further depression. It is my contention that both psychotherapy and medication are usually necessary for an effective intervention.

Theological Discourse and Women's Bodies

Theologically, again, we have some problems. A troublesome strand of Christian theology is the problem of dualism. Rosemary Radford Ruether points out that the problem with dualism is that women are placed in the undervalued half of the duo. The dualism runs like this:

male	female
white	black
good	evil

reason   emotion
spirit   body
control   chaos

Women are associated with embodiment, evil, and chaos, the "lesser" of the two halves. This dualistic strand in Christian theology has, unfortunately, been in an unholy alliance with what I have been calling the "truth-of-woman" discourse of the dominant culture, the discourse that disempowers, devalues, and denigrates women.[26]

The work of Michel Foucault again becomes helpful at this point. He speaks of discourse written on bodies. "The body manifests the *stigmata* of past experience. . . . The body is the *inscribed* surface of events . . . [the] task is to expose a body totally *imprinted* by history."[27] He speaks of the body being shaped by multiple regimes, as well as offering resistance. "The body is molded by a great many distinct regimes; it is broken down by the rhythms of work, rest, and holidays; it is poisoned by food or values, through eating habits or moral laws; it constructs resistances."[28]

This notion of bodies and power is also developed in Foucault's *Discipline and Punish* where he speaks of "the way in which the body itself is invested by power relations."[29]

> [T]he body is also directly involved in a political field; power relations have an immediate hold upon it; they invest it, mark it, train it, torture it, force it to carry out tasks, to perform ceremonies, to emit signs.[30]

The knowledge and control of the body he calls "the political technology of the body."[31]

One can speak of depression in women as their bodies bearing the "stigmata" of oppression. One can describe the bodies of depressed women as being "inscribed" by patriarchy, by the regime of the truth-of-woman discourse. Women's bodies are "imprinted, molded, broken down" by patriarchal discourse in many ways, and depression is one of them. Foucault refuses to allow us to relegate depression to the realm of the psychological, or even the interpersonal. His theory insists that we view women's depression as damage to women's bodies. This damage is part of a larger web that includes the social and psychological and ideational and institutional, but it must also include the effects on women's bodies.

Susan Bordo, in her work appropriating Foucault for feminism, has given a fascinating account of how the prevalence of eating disorders among women is an example of patriarchal discourse inscribed on women's bodies.[32] Cultural discourse regarding women's bodies, generating the desire to be small, to occupy a minimal amount of space, to be thin, is inscribed on the emaciated bodies of women with anorexia nervosa. Bordo describes how women with anorexia nervosa report a feeling of power and control over their body and its hunger, its desire to eat. In a world where they believe they have little power, they at least have a sense of mastery over their bodies. Of course it is a tragic form of illusory power, because it often becomes destructive to the point of starvation. Bordo makes the chilling point that these starving bodies are the imprint, the stigmata, of patriarchy on women.

I believe depression is also the imprint of patriarchy on women's bodies. Depression is a physiological manifestation of women's powerlessness. This cannot be argued at an individual level, that is, it is too simple to say that if a woman experiences powerlessness she gets depressed, or that powerlessness is the direct cause of an individual woman's episode of depression. After all, though all women are subject to patriarchal power, many women are not depressed, and many men are depressed. Rather, one can speak of this inscription of patriarchy on the *corporate body* of women as a way of accounting for the disproportionately high number of depressed women. While men and women may be equally biologically vulnerable to depression, powerlessness befalls women more than men, and this accounts for the disparate incidence of depression. While the horrifying pictures of women victims of battering, and the violation wrought by rape, the lack of resources for a safe abortion, and the daily deprivation of adequate nutrition and housing wrought by poverty are more obvious forms of damage to women's bodies, depression is a more invisible form of injury, yet one that must also be included in this list of physically damaging aspects of patriarchal truth-of-woman discourse. The challenge to Christian theology is to expose how strands of dualism contribute to this damaging discourse.

The Body and Spirituality

Many disciplines are beginning to overcome dualism by developing an understanding of the importance of spiritual well-being for physical well-being. More and more literature in nursing, medicine, gerontology, and public health is recognizing that prayer, meditation, and active church involvement are good for our bodies. This understanding of spirituality begins with "spirit" and names its intimate connection to the "body," thus helping to overcome debilitating views that separate the two. However, some of the current ways of talking about the interconnection can lapse into a spirit-body hierarchy that suggests that communion with the divine must always begin with the inner world or the psychic, while the body tags along behind. It is critical that we further the process of overcoming dualism by also viewing the body as a starting point for communion with God. This communion can take several forms.

Our bodies can be the starting point for *connection* to other people, creating the arena for communion with God. Losing oneself in intimate sexual relations can lead to a deep and sacred communion. Dance in pairs or in community can be another form of connection. Any one who has been to a celebration in Middle Eastern, African, Eastern European, or Jewish traditions knows the community building power of dance. The Chasid dances in defiance of God, as a form of praise as well as a form of rebellion against evil.[33]

The body can also be a source of *knowledge* of God. Out of the rigorous discipline of classical dance, whether it is Western ballet, Indian *bharata natyam,* or Japanese *kabuki* dance, this discipline can lead to a form of body knowledge beyond what we can think or meditate our way to. The regular discipline of running or biking or walking can also be an avenue to the sacred. If we take the incarnation seriously, that God indeed became flesh, then the flesh as one path to the knowledge of the divine must be considered.

The body is also a source of *pleasure.* Pleasure and bodies and God are three loci that have not traditionally connected in Christian piety, yet we can reclaim physical pleasure as a form of communion with the divine in our affirmation of the Word made flesh. Again, sexual expression not only connects us deeply to one another but gives us exquisite pleasure. Sensual delights in the form of touch, massage, or hot mineral springs are highly pleasurable. The scriptures are no stranger to connections of sensuality and spirituality: "Let him kiss me with the kisses of his mouth! For your love is better than wine, your anointing oils are fragrant, your name is perfume poured out" (Song of Sol. 1:2). Food and its tastes, textures, temperatures, and presentation are both pleasurable and associated with the presence of the divine. "Oh taste and see that God is good . . ." "People will come from east and west and south and north to sit at table with our Lord . . . Take, eat, this is my body. . . . This is the *joyful feast* of the people of God." The breaking of bread together is an affair of our physical bodies as well as the body of Christ. What is the boundary between praise and pleasure? It is not one that can be rigidly drawn as fully embodied creatures.

Our bodies are also a reminder of our *mortality.* We are nowhere more faced with our finitude than when we become aware of the fragility of our bodies. Illness, aging, and accident can all serve as reminders of our living day to day by the grace of God. This awareness of mortality can draw us into deeper solidarity with all of humanity who share this condition. We recognize that we are all "here but for a moment" and equal in our fragility.

Not only do our bodies remind us that we share mortality with the rest of humanity; they can also be the source of *solidarity* with suffering humanity. Bodies have been at risk in the ministries of accompaniment in El Salvador, when Salvadoran justice makers have been literally accompanied by North Americans so that they will be less vulnerable to government-related death squads. Anyone who has worked with people with infectious diseases, or done research on the virulent viruses, also risks bodily harm for the sake of the suffering. Anyone who has risked her or his life for another knows how bodies can be points of solidarity with the vulnerable ones of the earth.

The debilitating dualism of Christian tradition can be healed by seeing our bodies not only as interconnected with our spirits, but also as points of connection to God. The body/spirit that we are allows us to explore the fullness of embodiment as a way of communing with God.[34] We can celebrate our bodies as sources of connection, pleasure, knowledge, equality, and solidarity. We celebrate as beings formed from the dust of the earth in this creation that God declared good.

Chapter Seven

Anger

Anger is a familiar associate of depression. Where there is one, you will often find the other. What role does anger play in the genesis of depression? What role does anger play in the deconstruction of depression? What is the origin of the anger? Why is it there in the first place? The feminist answer always includes mention of a sexist cultural context. This chapter will explore the relationships among sexism, anger, depression, and power. It brings cognitive therapy approaches to the discussion and concludes with a pastoral counseling approach based on the language, idiom, and commitments of Christian tradition.[1]

Anger and Depression

Self-Directed Anger?

"Depression is anger turned inward," one of my students declared to me confidently. There is widespread belief that this is a reliable shorthand explanation for depression. Depression, according to this view, happens when an angry person cannot or will not express anger toward its appropriate object. The result is that the anger remains "bottled up" inside and therefore the object of the anger becomes the self. This view suggests that the depressed person is also secretly a hostile person, and in our culture, hostility means "not nice." It also suggests an immaturity in being able to handle conflict, interpersonal relationships, and the inevitable irritations and frustrations in human life. Of course, there are good reasons for this to be the popular assumption. It is rooted in perfectly respectable psychoanalytic thought. The field of pastoral counseling has also picked up on this as an accepted "fact" about depression. The *Dictionary of Pastoral Care and Counseling* reports, "Much of what people call depression is believed to be anger turned upon oneself."[2]

The psychoanalytic accounts say that the anger in depression is a response to loss. Whenever a person loses a significant object, Freud says, there is a mixture of love for the lost person and anger with that person over her or his abandonment. The libidinal energy, a mixture of love and anger, that was directed outwardly to this love object becomes transferred to the ego in an attempt to incorporate the lost object into the self. Depression is the result of this anger turned toward the ego. Freud summarizes the course of the injury to the ego after an object has been lost.

> [After the object loss] the free libido was not displaced on to another object; it was withdrawn into the ego. There, however, it was not employed in any unspecified way, but served to establish an *identification* of the ego with the abandoned object. Thus the shadow of the object fell upon the ego, and the latter could henceforth be judged by a special agency, as though it were an object, the forsaken object. In this way an object-loss was transformed into an ego-loss and the conflict between the ego and the loved person into a cleavage between the critical activity of the ego and the ego as altered by identification.[3]

Freud explains the role of loss, claiming that loss is at the heart of both grief and depression. According to Freud, "the exciting causes due to environmental influences are, so far as we can discern them at all, the same for both conditions."[4] Yet, in grief, "the disturbance of self-regard is absent."[5] The source of the self-loathing in depression is that anger directed toward one's own ego.

> The melancholic displays something else besides which is lacking in mourning—an extraordinary diminution in his self-regard, an impoverishment of his ego on a grand scale. In mourning it is the world which has become poor and empty, in melancholia it is the ego itself.[6]

In this description of the distinctiveness of melancholia, Freud gives a poignant rendering of the particular pain that is depression. The anger against the lost object is redirected against the ego. It is the resulting injury to the ego, manifest in an "extraordinary diminution in his self-regard," that is depression.

Anger and Helplessness

I depart from this widely accepted notion that depression is anger turned inward, in two ways. First, I prefer to think of anger as "often present" with depression, but not always, and usually present in complicated ways. Second, the anger in depression is not necessarily directed against the self. More likely, it is *ineffectual* anger, not *self-directed* anger, that gives rise to depression. Anger that has been frustrated, that has not been heeded and heard, is at the heart of depression. It is the repeated experience of futile anger that has not been able to change unacceptable circumstances that is depressogenic. In other words, it is the powerlessness, the impotence, the inefficacy that results in depression, not the anger. Anger is often an appropriate response to a bad situation. The angry person who, for whatever reason, is not able to change the bad situation will experience powerlessness, and depression can result. But that does not mean that the anger is redirected against the self. In depression, the anger has not changed its target; rather, the angry person has been unable to experience efficacy vis-à-vis the target. The original object of anger has not been replaced by the ego; rather, the depressed person feels helpless in making changes with regard to the object. It is the helplessness, the powerlessness, that is a trigger to depression, not anger turned toward the self.

For example, a woman comes to see you depressed, and you believe it is because of an intolerable work situation. Sexual harassment was a part of her daily work atmosphere. She had attempted to address the problem by speaking with the offender, appealing to superiors, looking for another job, avoiding contact, all to no avail. The chronic humiliation continued. She had resigned herself to the situation, believing that she had no choice. She seems to be mired in a bitter resignation. Her frustration over her inability to make changes eventually rendered her depressed. She was angry, but not at herself. Her anger has remained directed at her work circumstances. She remains angry about the harassment and has become depressed as a result of her sense of powerlessness.

Anger is a response to real or perceived helplessness. When one believes there are no options, that one is stuck, or if one has constructed a world which blocks a view of options, anger is often the response. Of course, not all helplessness is simply perceived, or inaccurately perceived. In other words, helplessness is not confined to the mind of the depressed beholder, particularly if that person belongs to a group that has traditionally been denied power. There are situations when options are in fact severely limited, where possibilities are constricted, and there are no good solutions. Anger is often appropriate and the prelude to a constructive response within the unchangeable parameters of the situation. When this anger is unheeded, frustrated, the risk for depression increases.

The anatomy of anger and depression, involving a complex interaction of many factors, is difficult to sort out. One of the factors is the instigating injury, which may be chronic or acute. This injury gives rise to the emotional response of anger. In response to this anger, if a woman perceives she is powerless to stop the injury, fails to take action, and the injury continues, she is at risk for depression. In addition, if she does not believe she is powerless and she responds to her anger by taking action, but in fact is powerless to stop the injury, again she is at risk for depression. On the other hand, if she experiences her action as effective in stopping the injury, depression is unlikely. This is a highly simplified analysis, one that does not take into account the many forms of resistance and survival mechanisms that women in conditions of oppression have developed to protect their mental health. What may appear to be inaction is in fact a subtle form of resistance. What may appear to be submission to chronic injury is in fact a way to survive intractable oppressive circumstances. These factors appear in many different forms and the patterns of interaction differ among individuals, ethnic groups, and social situations. It is not necessary to pinpoint an exact diagram of the interactions. It is enough to name these factors so that the discerning counselor or pastor can raise appropriate questions. What has the injury, chronic or acute, been? How is the individual interpreting the injury, and is it useful or dysfunctional? Is the person responding to the anger with constructive action or disempowering inaction? Has there been a depressed mood, and how is that affecting cognitive assessment and ability to act? These questions provide helpful therapeutic directions for inquiry; they do not constitute a model to apply to all people in all situations.

Anger as a Resource
for Depressed People

Rather than seeing anger as the result of individual inability to correctly "deal with" it, and therefore an indication of psychological underdevelopment, I believe anger is a healthy indication that something is wrong. One therapist explains it as like a red light that appears on the dashboard of the car. The signal is very useful, indicating that action needs to be taken to fix something. Furthermore, it is a car's well-functioning electrical system that will accurately report that something is wrong. The dangerous situation is when there is no red light to indicate a problem. Beverly Harrison says, "[Anger] is better understood as a feeling-signal that all is not well in our relation to other persons or groups or to the world around us."[7]

In addition to functioning as a signal, anger provides a source of energy for the change that needs to happen. Harrison describes "the power of anger in the work of love," stating that "Where anger rises, there the energy to act is present; . . . where feeling is evaded, where anger is hidden or goes unattended, masking itself, there the power of love, the power to act, to deepen relation, atrophies."[8] Even our bodies tell us that anger is a source of energy. The physiological mobilization of fight-or-flight resources are often a part of an angry reaction. The increased heart rate, dilated pupils, and sweat are stimulated by a rush of epinephrine into the bloodstream, all of which prepare the person to protect life, limb, and loves. For the depressed person anger is a sign of life. Anger is a sign that all is not lost to resignation, that there remains in the recesses of the psyche a residue of indignation that one's circumstances are wrong, unfair, and that something should be done about it. Anger is a sign that the rebellion is not dead.

Finally, anger is an indication that there is present a cognitive set that one has been wronged, that things are not right. As Beverly Harrison says, "[A]nger is—and always is—a sign of some resistance in ourselves to the moral quality of the social relations in which we are immersed."[9] This resistance is an extremely helpful resource in the treatment of depressed women. Theoretically speaking, if no anger is present, that indicates that there are no internal standards of self-worth, justice, or right and wrong that have been violated. Angry people are those who feel that they have been treated wrongly, that they deserve better. This is a healthy sign. The caregiver can take note that there are beliefs and assumptions that justice is one's due. This is a resource for countering negative self-statements. Therefore when the caregiver is aware of angry feelings in a parishioner, this is a hopeful sign. There are inner resources to be evoked in service of a more positive view of self and making important changes.

Audre Lorde, in describing her anger against racism, says, "My response to racism is anger. I have lived with that anger, ignoring it, feeding upon it, learning to use it before it laid my visions to waste, for most of my life."[10] "Learning to use [anger] before it laid my visions to waste" describes what is at stake in dealing with anger—it can lay waste to our visions.

Social Context of Women's Anger

The frequency of the occurrence of anger with depression is particularly interesting when one considers that there is a great deal for women to be angry about. This should be no surprise in a cultural milieu that diminishes women's worth. The focus of attention in the therapeutic literature has moved away from simply "getting in touch with your anger," away from finding ways to freely vent one's anger, like the primal scream therapies of the past. More and more, attention is being given to addressing the social and cultural circumstances that give rise to anger in the first place. Certainly, being aware of one's anger is important, and finding ways to express it in a clear and powerful way is important. But the events that lead up to its advent, the events in interpersonal relationship or in the public arena or in family of origin or in participation in the dominant culture, all of these are very important objects of attention for the person interested in addressing women's anger.

From a family systems perspective, it is the change in the relationship system that is therapeutic, not the mere expression of anger. Lerner states:

In sum, depression is not anger turned inward, although the denial of anger and lack of awareness of its sources can reinforce depression and mitigate against effective action. *Clinical depression and chronic anger and bitterness occur together, often signaling the necessity for change in a relationship system that is unconsciously viewed as lacking the flexibility to tolerate that change.*[11]

Simply an expression of anger is inadequate. Lerner believes that this venting is often already happening in many depressed women. Screaming, fighting, or blaming scenes often precede an episode of depression. Unless the expression of anger leads to a significant change in the relationship system, it does not address the source of the rage or the depression. Lerner notes, "Feelings of depression, low-self-esteem, self-betrayal, and even self-hatred are inevitable when women *fight but continue to submit* to unfair circumstances."[12] In other words, the tea kettle analogy does not work. In this mechanistic view, anger builds up steam in the boiling psyche which can be released by opening the lid and letting off steam. This view pays no attention to whether the expression of anger changes the cause of the anger; ignores the effect on the hearer, who may have nothing to do with the cause; and discounts the possibility that the hearer may react with double the aggression in return. Simply releasing anger is an inadequate answer.

Like all emotions, anger is socially constructed. Anger is not the result of internally generated psychic energy, like steam in a tea kettle. Anger is a result of cultural context and labels culled from personal and social history. A person is angry because the social context enables it, and provides the cognitive set, the beliefs and assumptions, the interpretive grid, rendering anger the appropriate response. Therefore to simply vent anger is not to dissipate it. As Carol Tavris says, "talking out an emotion doesn't reduce it, *it rehearses it.*"[13] Venting or talking at great length about one's anger is to reinforce it, not to reduce it. Perseverating on one's anger, expressing it *without changing the factors that gave rise to it,* simply reinforces the socially constructed cognitive set that made it possible.

What is at the heart of the anger in women's depression? Greenspan, a psychoanalytically oriented therapist, takes a cultural perspective and begins her discussion with a strong statement:

> [W]ithin many female psychological symptoms lies the seed of *unconscious rage at male domination.* This is nowhere more obvious than in the case of women who suffer from depression.[14]

At the heart of women's anger is rage over patriarchy.

While some feminists, like Greenspan, reveal a psychoanalytic orientation by pointing to internalized anger as the source of depression, they expand on the analytic view by placing anger in social context. This rage has its origins in women's subordinate status and unequal access to power, the "unconscious rage at male domination." In this situation of oppression, rage is not only likely but almost inevitable. Anger is the appropriate, healthy response to all the overt and covert messages of inferiority that women receive in patriarchal culture.

Like Lerner and Tavris, Greenspan believes that simply expressing anger is not enough. Women must learn that "fighting depression . . . [means] fighting back."[15]

> Curing women's depression is a matter of helping women *to understand the rage inside our depressions in terms of our oppression,* so that we can use it on our own behalf, even after we have expressed it in therapy.[16]

While Lerner speaks of making specific changes in family systems and marital relationships, Greenspan's suggestions are more political and communal. She speaks of the need to change legislation, family structure, work patterns, childcare, institutional power systems, and so forth. She also speaks of the need to speak freely and openly with other women who have experienced similar forms of subordination. The kind of validation, nurture, and support that is possible in all-women groups is invaluable in learning to claim a rightful place in the world. She also speaks of the need for some women to go though a stage of universalized anger, anger at both appropriate and inappropriate objects. This is a mobilizing phase, a way to escape the idea that women do not have permission to be angry, the fear, when women are angry, "that we look silly or frightened or ugly; that we are acting like bitches, dykes, or witches."[17] However, again she states that "anger is necessary, but anger is not enough."[18] In this treatment of anger she both appropriates and modifies classical Freudian connections between anger and depression.

Some who write in the area of cognitive therapy see anger as the result of frustrated sense of entitlement, and if there is a "problem" with anger, it is because of an inflated sense of what one is entitled to.[19] The solution, therefore, is to reduce your expectations of what is your due. The feminist perspective on this would be, yes, there is a frustrated sense of entitlement in anger, and rightly so! Anger is a justified and healthy response to the frustration of an appropriate belief about what one is entitled to, not an unhealthy response to a grandiose sense of entitlement.

The social context, both interpersonal and cultural, is critical for an understanding of women, depression, and anger. Audre Lorde gives us hope when she tells us that

> Every woman has a well-stocked arsenal of anger potentially useful against those oppressions, personal and institutional, which brought that anger into being. Focused with precision it can become a powerful source of change. And when I speak of change, I do not mean a simple ability to smile or feel good. I am speaking of a basic and radical alteration in those assumptions underlining our lives.[20]

This statement about a "well-stocked arsenal of anger" is suggestive of Foucault's statement that, in every place of hegemonic power, at the interstitial, local levels, there are also resistances. Lorde's statement suggests that resistance takes the form of anger, "a powerful source of change" that brings "radical alteration in those assumptions underlining our lives." We can be encouraged that women continue to be angry against oppressions in their lives, and we can, as pastoral caregivers, help them to harness this potentially creative power.

A word of caution is in order. It is important that we carefully guide our clients who are novices in the uses of anger. While feelings of anger are a source of power, expressions of anger can be a form of vulnerability. Therefore anger freely expressed can be a form of intimacy, a form of vulnerable communication of deepest feelings, and therefore a way of connecting to a loved one. It requires a context of trust that one will not be punished or shamed for such vulnerability. In a context of power disparities, on the other hand, the angry woman must learn how to use her anger strategically. For example, a vocal display of rage before superiors in the workplace, even if justified, can not only be ineffective, but can also be a pretext for being labeled immature, too emotional, out of control, and so forth. She must learn to use her anger as a motivation, as a fund for resistance, as a way of connecting with and organizing others in a similar position. While a brief temper tantrum can be a useful moment in a longer process of working out conflict between equal intimates, it can be detrimental to careful strategizing in addressing institutional injustice. An understanding of anger's context is critical for discerning anger's uses.[21]

Christian Theology and Women's Anger

"Many Christians put anger in the same category as lying, stealing, cheating, and using profanity. . . . [I]t seems to travel . . . in the wrong company—violence, fighting, yelling, and punishment, for example."[22] In addition to this astute statement about anger, Andrew Lester has accurately described reasons Christians feel guilty about being angry: "(1) social expectations to be 'nice,' (2) bad experiences with anger, and (3) Christianity's idea that anger is bad."[23] This last statement regarding "Christianity's idea" is important to explore. Lester reminds us of Ephesians 2:14 which speaks of the "dividing wall of hostility" that separates us from God.[24] He calls our attention to the unequivocal words of Jesus in Matthew 5:22: "But I say to you that if you are angry with a brother or sister, you will be liable to judgment." In traditional church lists of the seven deadly sins, anger is one of them. While it can be argued that these do not at all represent the whole of the scriptural or traditional views of anger in our Christian heritage, they tend to predominate in popular notions that anger is "unchristian."

While these three reasons apply to both men and women, they mesh neatly with the conditions of patriarchy to make it especially difficult for women to claim their anger. Cultural pressure to "be nice" is stronger for women than for men; the prevalence of domestic violence against women means women have good reasons to fear male anger; cultural notions of the feminine as compliant and pleasing mean the angry woman is a bad woman. These Christian texts and traditions, along with Christian suspicion of the passions, including anger, coalesce with sexist notions that women's passions, especially their anger, are dangerous. Or, another way to put it, women and the passions have been associated with the "lower" half of a dualistic world, while men and reason are associated with the "upper" half. So how can the feminist theologian rethink anger?

Beverly Harrison's work provides a starting point. She describes anger as "not the opposite of love," but as a "mode of connectedness to others that is always a vivid form of caring." She states, "Extreme and intense anger signals a deep reaction to the action upon us or toward others to whom we are related."[25] Theologian Elizabeth Johnson describes "the righteous anger that waxes hot because something good is being violated." She reminds us that this anger "gives birth to courage and humor and unleashes energy for change."[26] Johnson goes on to give us a startling and exhilarating image of God: "Women ablaze with righteous anger."[27] Moving from women's wrath to God's wrath, she reclaims images of the wrath of God from Hebrew scriptures.

> The righteous symbol of divine wrath discloses God's outrage at the harm done to those she loves: this should not be. True, God's anger lasts but a moment; true, it is always instrumental, aimed at change and conversion. But it stands as an antidote to sentimentality in our view of God's holy mystery as love, and as a *legitimation of women's anger at the injustice of their own diminishment and the violation of those they love*.[28]

So she brings the circle back to women. "Women ablaze with righteous anger" becomes a metaphor for God's wrath in scriptures, and God's wrath in scriptures becomes a legitimation of women's anger over injustice of all sorts.

Depression as Strategy?

Can an episode of depression itself be an expression of anger? Can it be a form of resistance fueled by rage? Miriam Greenspan has an interesting analysis of depression as a "strategy" for women, one that indirectly serves a woman's purposes.[29] She sees some depressions as a form of passive-aggressive resistance to male domination.

The hidden protest in depression, the submerged message of resistance is: "I'm determined to be miserable and mean and depressed, no matter what you say or do. You're not good or wise or strong enough to help me, try as you will." There is an unmistakable though extremely indirect challenge to authority in depression. Strategically, it allows the Woman as Victim to make herself feel more powerful, by making the other feel less powerful.[30]

This form of resistance, this "hidden protest in depression," occurs partly because women are not usually taught to be direct in stating our wishes, anger, dissenting views. Women have also adopted this mode because "*indirect power exerted on men often works* where direct power will not—as any woman knows, who has ever cried (rather than argued) to get her way."[31]

This interesting line of argument highlights the desperation that some women feel and the lengths to which some women will go to accommodate to cultural sanctions against female anger while still registering a protest. What could be more desperate and tragic than choosing mental illness as the only way to be heard? However, it is a risky line of argument. It leaves women open to the accusation that "she wants attention, she is pouting, she is acting like a child, she just won't try, won't be a good sport, won't do her part." Women are often blamed for their unhappiness. "It is her own fault." Greenspan's point does call attention to the fact that women do have some measure of control over depression, that women have some choices over how to register protest and seek change. Will it be through passive-aggressively becoming depressed or by making direct moves toward change? Yet this important point about women's agency can easily become a stance that blames the victim. I would use caution at this juncture in appropriating Greenspan's views.

Pastoral Counseling of Angry Depressed Women

Several attitudes toward anger can be discerned. When caregivers sense anger in a parishioner, they can discern what is the status of a woman's anger.

1. Perhaps the most heartbreaking is the woman who is very depressed and locked in an internal world of despair. You as the counselor know of her life circumstances, and you know that there are many things in her life that might make a person very angry: chronic mistreatment at home, underpayment at work, a past with many hurts and humiliations, for example. Yet she reports no anger; you sense only resignation and hopelessness. At this level, any sign of anger is welcome, because it is a sign of life, a sign of rebellion. While sensitive therapists will not attempt to argue with a woman's reports

that she is not angry, they can watch for openings, cracks in the firmly rooted beliefs that are rendering anger absent, or inaccessible. A clenched jaw when speaking of experiences of childhood verbal abuse, a flat affect when speaking of her distant husband, shoulders stiff when describing conditions at work—these are openings to hidden anger. These physical features can be gently and nonjudgmentally noted. The client can then be invited to reflect on their meaning. The pastoral counselor can try to create some cognitive dissonance by checking for a "double standard." Ask her how she would feel if someone else, a sister or good friend for example, were treated the same way. Would she be angry on their behalf? Another possibility is speculating that you, the counselor, would likely feel angry under those circumstances. This can offer an alternative, legitimate emotional response to her difficult life. Try to discern the underlying beliefs and assumptions that are behind her flat affect. Does she truly believe that she is being treated justly? What is the meaning scheme behind her lack of anger? She may say, "I am a lazy worker and an inadequate wife who deserves mistreatment." Or, "This is not mistreatment, this is the way women's lives are." The therapist can begin to slowly question these meaning schemes. The goal, at this level, is to enable a woman to feel her feelings.

2. "I'm not angry," she states with a smile that looks more like a grimace. Yet the grimace speaks louder than her words, and her fists are clenched, her neck muscles are protruding, her face is flushed. Your intuition tells you that a more accurate statement might be, "I desperately don't want to be angry because nice Christian women are never angry." It does not take much reflection for her to realize that, yes, there are many things she is angry about. "But," you may hear, "I have learned to deal with my anger. I just leave the room for a few minutes and soon it is gone." This is a woman who knows she is angry, but is trying very hard to hide it from herself and from you. You sense she is deeply ashamed of her anger. Some women who hate their anger believe it is unjustified, that their anger is a sign of personal sinfulness. Other women who hate their anger believe it is justified, but that they should "rise above it," knowing life isn't perfect. Their anger is a sign of personal immaturity. Justified or not, their anger is bad.

At this level of awareness, cognitive therapy techniques can be helpful as a way to change a woman's attitude toward anger. The counselor can point out places in scripture where God was angry for righteousness' sake. The many characters in scripture who have been angry on behalf of the poor and oppressed, or even angry with God, can be invoked. Anger can be interpreted as useful in at least two ways: one, as a signal system, a helpful sign that something is wrong and a call to make changes; two, as an energy source, as what gets you moving and keeps you moving when the personal and social inertia is great. It is also helpful to distinguish between feelings and behavior. Anger that one acknowledges is different from anger that is accompanied by violent behavior. Often anger is assumed to be completely uncontrollable and destructive. A reminder about the difference between feelings and action is important. At this stage, the goal is to reframe anger as an emotion that is helpful for several reasons, and one that is consistent with scripture.

If this is a woman who has never expressed her anger to its outermost limits, who has never had the experience of raging at life and death, love and hate, good and evil and the universe, it may be helpful for her to find a safe place to do that. She may need to know that she can feel and express her anger at its heights and depths before another *and she will not be abandoned.* If it is fear of rejection that is at the heart of her fear of her anger, she may need to inhabit her anger fully in the presence of a trustworthy person in order to be convinced that she is still loved, anger and all. This is risky counsel to give, because you as caregiver do not know for certain that the listener, if it is not yourself, is trustworthy. But the effect of a woman traveling into the bowels of her rage before another, and being accepted nevertheless, is a tremendous experience of grace.

The woman who has lived in shame and hiding because of her angry feelings may go through a period of free-floating anger. It is expressed in appropriate and inappropriate places, at justified and unjustified objects, and in helpful and unhelpful ways. She is in the process of learning the contours of her feelings as well as a repertoire of new behaviors. She may be neither skilled nor graceful in these early days of awareness of her anger. But neither will she be mired in a disabling self-hatred, a resignation to her circumstances, and a depression unchallenged. This phase will require patience from counselor, friends, and family. If necessary, the caregiver may need to reinterpret their friend, mother, wife, or loved one to those who are bewildered and hurt by these new behaviors.

3. At a very different place is the woman who is already freely expressing her anger, but in a very ineffectual way. She may believe that venting her anger is healthy. This may be the outcome of widespread belief that "stuffing your anger down," or "stifling your rage" or "repressed feelings" are the source of mental and physical illness. Or she may not believe that her anger is healthy, but she has found that it is the only way to get anyone's attention. Everyone feels horribly wounded and exhausted afterwards, but at least she has communicated that the dirty laundry is to be put in the clothes hamper. Whatever the reason, this woman engages in screaming, throwing tantrums that, if the truth be told, do not serve anyone well.

Unlike the woman in the previous example, she does have the active expression of anger in her behavioral repertoire. But she needs the additional interpretation of her anger not only as calling for free expression but as calling for change: things need to change because something is wrong. "You bet something is wrong," she may reply; "the laundry is in the wrong place!" A closer examination will show that this is not the only thing that is wrong; there are other family habits that are wrong as well. The change that is needed may be in family patterns of interaction. She may need assertiveness skills, communication skills, or conflict resolution skills. The family system may need to change, requiring a reordering of the family roles, rules, and rituals.[32] The critical task for the therapist is to discern what is wrong, and then to enable the woman, and if necessary her family, to make changes.

If resistance to change is strong, you may need to address the hopelessness and powerlessness. Many women are well aware that something is wrong, but their assessment of the situation is that it is hopeless, nothing will ever help, and things won't really change. Cognitive therapy again becomes a useful way to challenge distortions regarding the possibility of change. Certainly cognitive therapy will not, in a truly naive and falsely optimistic way, suggest that the changes will be easy or quick. Some of the changes may be disruptive, disorienting, and painful for many people involved. It may feel like a cruel thing to do to the family, or it may feel horribly uncertain and anxiety producing. The counselor can interpret these as accurate descriptions of the situation: yes, change is often painful and scary. But the alternative was to be chronically angry and depressed. The counselor can provide support and reassurance as difficult changes are made.

4. Another type of woman may come to your door. She knows when she is angry; she knows anger is a useful emotion; she knows how to listen to anger as a call to make changes, and she has made many. Yet she is still troubled by her anger. You sense that there is another step she can take: she can direct the energy of her anger toward concerted action to change harmful, dehumanizing social structures. If anger is related to powerlessness, her anger may be related to her sense of powerlessness to do anything about suffering and injustice in the world. While we know that no one of us can change the world, it is not only good for the world but good for ourselves to engage in communal efforts to feed the hungry, clothe the naked, liberate the oppressed, welcome the stranger. An important part of a woman finding her power is in naming the social and cultural origins of her oppression, and in finding others who are engaged in changing these conditions. And, equally important, a woman who has found her power will address the corporate sources not only of her own oppression, but also of others' oppression, including those forms of oppression in which she participates as oppressor. As feminist Christians, we cannot be engaged in changing only our own personal and interpersonal circumstances. We must be about creating social and cultural conditions for human flourishing for all people. And we must be about the task of confessing and repenting of the ways we participate in and benefit from oppressive structures.

These four attitudes toward anger can be identified among women who struggle with depression. They fall roughly on a continuum from not feeling anger, to feeling anger but being ashamed of it, to recognizing the legitimacy of anger but not hearing it as a call to make changes, to hearing anger as a call to make changes in one's personal life but not yet as a call to engage in social change efforts. Ideally, a woman would recognize her anger, feel its currents physically and emotionally. She would hear it as a call to act, to make changes in the circumstances of her family life, the workplace, her intimate relationships. And she would see that anger at systems of oppression calls for organized, concerted action. As Helen Caldicott counseled in confronting despair, "Do something and do it together." It is this final stage of consciousness regarding anger that we as pastoral caregivers often omit, preferring to see our province as the intrapsychic, personal cognitive set, or marriage and family life. To fully address women's anger in the therapeutic context, this corporate action to make systemic changes must be included.

Chapter Eight

Hope

Help of the helpless, O abide with me.

—Henry F. Lyte[1]

So even I, and with a pang more thrilling,
So even I, and with a hope more sweet,
Yearn for the sign, O Christ, of Thy fulfilling,
Faint for the flaming of Thine advent feet.
—Frederick William Henry Myers[2]

God dwells in the details.

—Ludwig Mies van der Rohe

Hopelessness is the hallmark of depression. If there is one feature that defines the experience of depression, it is hopelessness. Almost all subjective descriptions of depression include it, almost all symptomatologies include it. William Styron describes the "unrelenting pain" in depression, but declares that "[i]t is hopelessness even more than pain that crushes the soul."[3]

Everyone knows what it is to have their hope challenged. I remember the hope that many of us had in seminary. In spite of predictions about the destruction of the environment, the feminization of poverty, and the population explosion, we believed we would make a difference. We hoped we would make a difference. Yet now, fifteen years later, most of the dire predictions have been realized. Our hopes were not fulfilled. In fact, there are new disasters that we could not have predicted, such as AIDS, and an increasingly passive consumer-like electorate, disengaged from active participation in shaping local and national political agendas. True, the bilateral arms race seems to have been arrested, but we have new post–Cold War problems: the eruption of ethnic hatred, the insidious proliferation of nuclear weapons and technology around the globe. Everyone who believes in and works for a better world, a more compassionate world, a world characterized by the love and justice of God in Jesus Christ, knows what it is to have hopes challenged.

Yet the hopelessness of the depressed is more sweeping than the hopelessness of the one who is not in the throes of depression. It is more global, more comprehensive. It vitiates love, motivation, self-care, feeling, action, relationship, work, creativity. Why love if there is no hope of it lasting, or being returned? Why take care of one's self with morning grooming or with pleasurable activities or improving one's life if it will all come to naught? Why work, or create, if it is all useless? The hopelessness of the depressed extends from beliefs about the minute details of personal hygiene to beliefs about international geopolitics, attitudes on subjects from daily menu to the fate of the universe itself. One woman spoke of a painful moment of depression when she stared at a sliced orange and thought, "Why bother with vitamin C, it really doesn't matter." The one who is discouraged, but not depressed, about family, the world, and the church can often find spheres of hope, dimensions of hope, where goodness continues to dwell, where love continues to be possible. Or, if the discouraged person has a bad night, or a bad week, the hopelessness will lift, to some extent, with time. The person who is depressed will find nothing hopeful, anywhere, ever. The unrelenting, global nature of the hopelessness is overwhelming.

Hope, Care, and Time

So how do we as carers for the depressed revive hope? Two pastoral theologians who have written recently about hope offer guidance. Their discussions are as rich theologically as they are therapeutically. They call attention to the fact that hope involves a particular orientation toward time.

Donald Capps speaks of giving hope by the "reframing of time," changing our perception of our past and our future.[4] He tells us reframing involves "placing a problem or difficulty within a new perceptual framework and thereby changing its meaning."[5] He offers the following illustration to explain the dynamics of reframing.

> There was a farmer in a poor country village. He was considered very well-to-do because he owned a horse that he used for plowing and transportation. One day his horse ran away. All his neighbors exclaimed how terrible this was, but the farmer simply replied, "Maybe."
>
> A few days later the horse returned and brought two wild horses with it. The neighbors all rejoiced at his good fortune, but the farmer simply replied, "Maybe."

The next day the farmer's son tried to ride one of the wild horses, but the horse threw him and broke the son's leg. The neighbors all offered their sympathy for his misfortune, but the farmer again replied, "Maybe."

The next week conscription officers came to the village to take young men for the army. They rejected the farmer's son because of his broken leg. When the neighbors told him how lucky he was, the farmer replied, "Maybe."[6]

Capps comments: "Having two wild horses is a good thing until it is seen in the context of the son's broken leg. Then, the broken leg seems to be bad in the context of peaceful village life; but in the context of conscription and war, it suddenly appears good."[7] The changed context transforms the belief about what is good and desirable. In this way, reframing is a powerful tool for transforming hopelessness into hopefulness.

To reframe the future, he describes a psychotherapeutic method that involves asking clients to imagine themselves in the hoped-for future, and then to describe the steps taken to arrive there.[8] This method is grounded in the belief that "we can have a different future from the one our present difficulties and problems would predict, and that we can take personal responsibility for effecting this alternative outcome."[9] This process unlocks visions of possibility that were precluded by the hopeless scenario that had prevailed. Furthermore, it helps people articulate specific steps to take to reach this hoped-for future. This can be both a motivating and a practical method, it can both engender hope and facilitate strategies for change.

Capps also speaks of reframing past history in terms of "revising the past."[10] Thus the past is always open to a new interpretation in the light of a present-day transformation. He makes the provocative claim that "the past is as open and possibility-filled as the future."[11] This is because "what is always open about the past is the meaning or significance we assign to it."[12] "Biographical rehabilitation" is a phrase he borrows to describe the reinterpretation of one's past in the presence of a gracious God.[13] He recognizes that the particular facts of the past cannot, of course, be altered, but the debilitating meanings attached to them can be changed in the therapeutic process. Therefore, for example, the person who believes they are forever burdened by sins committed in the past, or permanently damaged by victimization suffered in the past, can be given the gift of changing the meaning assigned to these events so that they do not define present possibilities. Revising the past, or biographical rehabilitation, is "grounded in the boundless mercy of God, who is able to take sinful actions that we and others committed in the past and make of them something better than we would ever have imagined."[14] Rendering both the future and the past possibility-filled is a powerful means of giving hope to the present moment.

These revisions of the past and the projected future carry important theological implications for Capps. God is the gracious one who not only opens the future, but is able to transform even a sinful past. "God is the original and eternally Hopeful Self, who uses the autonomy that is God's own to hold both past and future open for ever new possibilities."[15] Furthermore, not only our hoping, but our very existence is due to this "eternally Hopeful Self." In response to God's own need, God created the world "into which God's very self has been invested from the beginning until now and forever after." We can take from Capps the very powerful notion that the hope that compels us as caregivers, and that we seek to sustain in those for whom we care, is grounded in a God whose hopefulness we know by our very existence.

Andrew Lester gives us another way to offer hope through locating the depressed person in the context of a sacred narrative, one that opens the future to the grace and power of God. He speaks of "future stories," and how they offer hope.[16] He makes rich use of narrative theory which lifts up the "tensed" character of human life—the fact that we are located in past, present, and future tenses. Like Capps, he offers reframing techniques, which can "help people 'rearrange the furniture' and 'change the decorations' that make up a 'certain room' in their memory."[17] This process can transform a crippling past, invigorate the present, and offer hope for the future.

However, Lester points out that some lack any future story at all, and there is no future story to reframe. In these cases, a future story must be constructed. Whether reframing or constructing a future story, Lester presents several helpful techniques. One of them is storytelling about the future. This involves "imagin[ing] a future story that is good news, one that has them reaching positive values and experiencing a joyful life."[18] These stories can be evoked with such statements as the following:

> If your life was made into a wonderful movie with a happy ending, tell me what that last part of the movie would look like.
>
> If you wrote me a letter in a few years and it was filled with good news about your life, what would the letter say?[19]

These stories are useful because they can "serve as a basis for choosing creative behaviors, actualizing realistic possibilities, and adopting a more hopeful stance toward the future."[20] When the client cannot create a future story, the caregiver can construct one for her. This is a powerful activity because it "envision[s] the future beyond where a person's own imagination can take them."[21]

Such future stories provide fruitful resources for the caregiver seeking to use cognitive therapy to introduce a more hope-giving hermeneutic for a person's understanding of self, world, and future. Hope-giving involves working with memories of the past and expectations of the future to free the present for meaningful, fruitful choices.

Women Hopefully Speaking of God

Yet it seems to me that more must be said of hope when addressing the problem of depressed women. The hope that is required includes the courage to address principalities and powers that damage women's bodies and souls. Rebecca Chopp is one theologian who includes depression as a form of damage wrought by cultural and political oppression. She speaks of "psychic oppressiveness" that includes "failure, suicide, stress, psychosis, drug addiction, *depression*, and schizophrenia."[22] Not only is oppression manifest in the poverty and desolation of the "others" of history, but also in such disorders as depression as well. Chopp also named sources of hope in "forms of subversion."

> Furthermore, as discourses of freedom, proclamation must protest against oppressiveness and repressiveness though practices of insurrection, be they boycotts, prayers, fasts, alternative life-styles, legislative changes, or other forms of subversion. Issues such as nuclear destruction, *depression*, third world–first world relations, and aging all provide places to stand from which to capture a view of the social-symbolic order, places to render judgment in the midst of grace.[23]

Depression provides a "place to render judgment in the midst of grace." In the midst of the grace of oppression resisted, emancipation proclaimed, psyches healed, lives restored, there can be judgment rendered against all that would hinder such movements.

How do we speak of the God of hope while standing in this place of depression? There are several ways women who have known depression can speak of God. Sharon Welch articulates a radically immanent view of God. She begins by speaking of "love that gives birth to hope" and quotes Carter Heyward's understanding of God.[24]

> For god is nothing other than the *eternally creative source* of our relational power, our common strength, a god whose movement is to empower, bringing us into our own together, a god whose name in history is love— provided we mean by "love" not just simply a sentiment or unfocused feeling but rather that which is just, mutually empowering, and co-creative.[25]

Then she goes a step further than Carter Heyward.

> While Heyward claims that "god" is the source of our relational power, I argue that the divine *is* that relational power, and that it is neither necessary nor liberating to posit a substance or ground that exists outside of relational power.[26]

Later she speaks of "divinity as a quality of relationships, lives, events and natural processes."[27] She understands the divine to be radically immanent.

"Divinity, or grace, is the resilient, fragile, healing power of finitude itself."[28] While she emphasizes the immanence of God, she claims that there is also a transcendence associated with this God, in four ways. There is transcendence in the capacity to name the mysterious complexity of life, in the beauty and rhythms of nature, in love for life in spite of all that would squelch that love, and in social change movements.[29]

This radically immanent view of the God in whom we hope will speak to the experience of some depressed women. For those who have been unable to speak of any sort of transcendence, those for whom anything beyond the particularities of day-to-day survival have been rendered meaningless and irrelevant, this way of speaking of God will give hope. Their God has been known in that finite medication, human being, morning exercise, or crossword puzzle that has brought temporary relief from the pain, or longer-lasting cure for the disorder.

Other women will find that it is precisely hope in a powerfully transcendent God that has enabled survival. Hope lies in a memory of what this transcendent God has done. This is the hope of the prophets in the Hebrew scriptures, calling the faithful to remember the mighty acts of God in the past, and on the basis of that memory, have hope for the future. Hope lies in trusting that God will act in ways consistent with past actions. Hope is possible because of the continuity of the present and the future with the past. This kind of hope can be kindled in the depressed woman. Memories can be evoked of times of love, happiness, or creativity. Using cognitive therapy, these memories can be evoked as powerful challenges to the negative assessment of self, world, and future. The depressed person can be assured of a powerful God's sustaining presence in the past, a presence that has not deserted them.

However, this kind of hope may not be available to the one who is severely depressed. There are those whose depression obliterates access to any positive memories. The distorting effects of depression have obliterated any possibility for memory as a resource for hope. Another kind of hope in the Hebrew scriptures is appropriate in the case of the severely depressed. Rather than hoping in what God has already done, this is hope based on what God has not done yet. This is the hope based on God acting in ways never yet seen. This is the hope in apocalyptic literature. This hope is not based on continuity, but on discontinuity with the past. Communities that are experiencing tremendous suffering base their hope on God doing something radically new, something unimaginable. This is the hope that survives when the light seems to have been utterly extinguished. The woman who finds no basis for hope in her finite world, nor any grounds for hope in her memory, will cling to a hope in what is unseen and unimaginable.

Depressed women will not all find the same theological basis for hope. They will speak hopefully of God in different ways. They may speak of God in radically immanent ways or in traditionally transcendent terms. This diversity will be honored by the caregiver who seeks to engender hope among the hopelessness of depression.

Qualities of Hope

I would like to name five statements about hope that support the one struggling to "keep hope alive" (Jesse Jackson).

First, *hope is an action*. Hope is not confined to a feeling or an attitude. It is also a way of acting or behaving. It can involve acting in spite of a feeling of hopelessness, in spite of a sense of futility. It can be an action that is counterintuitive, an act that goes against all within us that tells us, "This is useless." Therefore it takes great courage to engage in this action called hope. It takes tremendous boldness to act in spite of one's feelings, instead of in accordance with them.

In the movie *Tender Mercies*, actor Robert Duvall plays a has-been country and western singer who was a recovering alcoholic who has lost his first love and his career, and the devastating blow was loss of his daughter in a fatal car accident. He was utterly defeated. The last scene takes place outside in the wide-open Texas plains, with the huge sky stretched out before us. The Duvall character is railing against the universe, decrying the hopelessness of life itself, the futility of it all. Yet all the while he is vigorously, even frantically, hoeing a garden. As he denounces all hopefulness, he acts with hope. He continues to tend the garden, even when feeling utterly defeated. This is the stance of the depressed person seeking hope: continuing to act with hope, even when feeling no hope. In the absence of feeling, intuition, or faint glimmers of possibility, the depressed person will continue to act with hope, continue to till the garden.

One of the difficult things about depression is that it clouds perceptions, distorts assessments, rendering feelings unreliable. Persons who usually have a reliable set of intuitions, ones that have guided them wisely in the past, will find upon becoming depressed that these intuitions have become so negatively distorted that they are no longer trustworthy sources of guidance. Therefore the depressed person will act with hope even when feeling no hope. The result can be not only the achievement of the hoped-for results but also the rebirth of a hopeful attitude. As is often stated in the course of cognitive therapy, actions often precede feelings. This is also true of hope.

Or, if hope is an action in spite of one's having no hopeful feeling, it may also be a response to another feeling, such as fear. Usually we do not applaud fear as a healthy reason to act. Fear suggests retreat, or cowardice. Yet even fear can give rise to an action worthy to be called hope. One woman described to me the extraordinary effect of regular aerobic exercise on her life.

Not only had she lost forty pounds but her mood had improved considerably. Whenever she felt her mood slipping, she would go running. It seemed to me the critical moment was when she actually chose to put on her running shoes, and walk out of the house, even though her mood had taken a downward turn. The tendency at that moment would be to give up, crawl in bed, flip on the TV—in other words, to acquiesce to the suggestions of the depressed mood. So I pressed her on what it was that made her actually act counter to that resignation, that impulse to give in to the mood. She said, "Fear." "Of what?" I asked. "Of not being alive." Whatever the feeling impulse to act hopefully, whether it is hope or fear or sheer cognitive willpower, the act itself can be considered hope, regardless of the feeling.

Second, *hope is specific.* Hope dwells in the details. The architect Ludwig Mies van der Rohe said of his creations that God dwells in the details. The same can be said of hope. It is our actions that seem very small that are hope. We can speak of hope for the world, for future generations, for our salvation, for the spread of the gospel to the ends of the earth. Yet hope must also dwell in the details. Hope that is detached from the mundane aspects of day-to-day living is not hope. It is wishful thinking. A powerful hope is one that is carried out in the myriad activities of the here and now. I believe parents know this well. While parents may have great hopes for their children's future health and happiness, they also know that hope is lived out by tending to runny noses, untied shoes, carpools, PTA meetings. A grand hope apart from this attention to details is no hope at all. Therefore hope is an action, and it includes action in the details of life.

Anne Lamott writes about hope that begins here and now, in the details.

> Thirty years ago my older brother, who was ten years old at the time, was trying to get a report on birds written that he'd had three months to write, which was due the next day. We were out at our family cabin in Bolinas, and he was at the kitchen table close to tears, surrounded by binder paper and pencils and unopened books on birds, immobilized by the hugeness of the task ahead. Then my father sat down beside him, put his arm around my brother's shoulder, and said, "Bird by bird, buddy. Just take it bird by bird."[30]

When we are overwhelmed, hope happens as we get started, bit by bit, bird by bird. Tending to the details is integral to hoping.

Third, *hope means patience.*[31] Adrienne Rich tells us, "A wild patience has brought me this far."[32] There is hardly serenity of soul or equanimity of spirit here. Rather this is a tough patience. A perseverance against the odds is suggested. This is a steadfastness that is characterized as "wild." Patience is not to give up, even when sorely tempted to. We will be tempted, Lord knows we will be tempted. Patience is the assurance that it is worth it, it is worth the frustration, worth the setbacks. In the words of a verse of "We are climbing Jacob's ladder," we hear, "The struggle's long, but hope is longer." We are reminded of the suffragettes singing, "We shall not, we shall not be moved, just like a tree that's planted by the water, we shall not be moved." Many of us are surprised to learn that the movement to secure the vote for women took seventy years. It was only a wild patience that kept such hope alive. Those of us who saw the movie *Gandhi*, which ended with independence for India, are surprised to realize that he worked for twenty years in South Africa for justice movements, and then thirty more years in India. It was not a matter of five or six years of commitment to justice, it was a matter of an entire adult lifetime. This is a wild patience.

The person who is depressed will require such patience, such perseverance, such hope against hope. Anne Lamott spoke of this patience when she wrote, "Hope begins in the dark, the stubborn hope that if you just show up, and try to do the right thing, the dawn will come. You wait and watch and work: You don't give up."[33] For many depressed people, it is precisely in the dark that hope begins. For many who are depressed, showing up and trying to do the right thing is the only way of accessing the realm of the hopeful. A dogged unwillingness to give up is all that sustains their hope. This doggedness is neither easy nor pleasant nor natural. It can feel uncomfortable, uncertain, foolish, and exhausting. Yet it is this refusal to give up that is at the heart of hope. To say, "hope begins in the dark" is not to say, "hope begins in the dark with only a tiny glimmer of light." It is to say, rather, that hope begins in the confusion, uncertainty, and insecurity of total darkness. Therefore, hope does not depend on sight, on glimpses, on glimmers. Rather, it depends on waiting, watching, and working.

Fourth, *hope is rebellious.* Hope is not a sweet optimism, nor is it a gentle placidity. I have spoken of hope as patience, meaning steadfastness, but I also want to speak of hope as impatience, meaning rebellion. Hope can also be a revolt against injustice, a revolt against pain and suffering, a revolt against all that would dehumanize another. In a heart-wrenching scene in *The Women of Brewster Place*, we see this kind of hopeful rebellion in a character called Mattie. Her young friend Ciel has just lost a young child. Ciel has not emerged from her room for days, she has not eaten or spoken to a soul. When Mattie, the matriarch of the community, visits her, she is horrified by the frail, withered figure that Ciel presents. From her lips comes a cry of both hope and rebellion.

> "Merciful Father, no!" she bellowed. There was no prayer, no bended knee or sackcloth supplication in those words, but a blasphemous fireball that shot forth and went smashing against the gates of heaven, raging and kicking, demanding to be heard.[34]

Then Mattie began the tender process of bringing Ciel back to life. This smashing against the gates of heaven is a rebellion that is an act of hope that precedes an act of restoration to the land of the living.

The depressed person can find great hope in revolt. This may be a crude and desperate act of defiance. Or it may appear to someone not depressed that it is a small act that would require little effort. Yet for the person who is depressed, who is struggling to engage in the palliative and healing activities required, small acts can feel huge. It may feel like a tremendous revolt against the powers of death and despair to simply get out of bed, dress, and go to the grocery store. The point is, the depressed person can be encouraged to engage in what feels like rebellion as a way to keep from being defeated by the inertia of depression. The therapist can reframe rebellion as something healthy, and not something that will invite punishment. The caregiver can instill a spirit of resistance to the debilitating mood. The depressed person can be challenged to defy the deadening effects of depression. Depressed persons can be encouraged to say *on their own behalf,* "Merciful God, no!" This can provide the impulse to stay alive, to continue to heal.

Fifth, *hope is communal.* We are not called to hope alone. We are not called to remain hopeful as solitary individuals. We are called to hope, just as we are called to be Christians: as a church. Therefore, when we cannot find it within us to hope, others will hope on our behalf. When we find it impossible to feel hope, to act with hope, to remain steadfast, others will do so on our behalf. Others will believe when we simply cannot. When we cannot pray, others will pray in our stead. The same is true of hope. Hope is a communal affair, a matter of the interdependent, mutually upbuilding members of the body of Christ. It is the body that hopes, not the individual members alone.

I remember the Easter season at Princeton Theological Seminary when the seminary holds a Paschal Vigil. Everyone gathers on the Saturday evening before Easter Sunday in the chapel at the center of campus. There the creation story is read. At the point that Adam and Eve are expelled from the garden, we are ushered out into the crisp night air to another place on campus, where the stories of the patriarchs and matriarchs are read. Then we move to another place where we share a seder meal, remembering and reenacting the exodus story. As the evening progresses, we realize that we are the people of God, moving through history, rehearsing the sacred story of scripture. The most moving portion of the evening for me is at the end. We have just celebrated the life, death, and resurrection of Jesus Christ, and we are moving back to the chapel, where the evening began, where our journey began. We are walking again, as a group, and we represent the era of the church moving through history. We are accompanied by huge banners of the saints of the church, Martin Luther, John Calvin, John Knox, Sojourner Truth, Martin Luther King Jr., Mother Teresa. But we can see up ahead, ablaze in light for the first time all evening, the chapel, to which we are returning. From its open doors pours triumphant Easter music, and we know that inside is a spectacular banner of the lion and the lamb dwelling together, representing the time when the whole will be fulfilled in the final triumph of God. But we are not there yet. We huddle together, the night having grown colder than ever. We have each other, we are accompanied by these saints, and we carry candles to light at least a little of the way. This is where we are as a church. Where do the depressed persons fit into this picture? They may be among the travelers, walking in the absence of hopeful feelings. Or they may have had to rest by the side of the road, letting others proceed when they cannot even walk. Or they may even be spectators from the windows as the procession passes by. But they see and hear the procession, they belong to the procession, they are included, even if they feel cut off from the hope, the community, the future glory.

Finally, a word of hope for the caregiver. It can be tremendously discouraging to work with someone whose depression is entrenched. It seems to be a thankless task to continue to care for someone who seems to remain unaffected by all our best efforts at love and relationship and care. Depression can be stubborn and can wear out even the most stubborn caregivers who take it on. We run out of words, stories, empathy. It is difficult to know what to say next that could possibly make a difference. At that point, we need to remind ourselves that we are engaged in a creative act, and creativity is difficult and painful, as well as absorbing and lifegiving. What Anne Lamott says about the creative, and often difficult, process of writing, could also be said about the often equally difficult task of caring for a depressed person.

> You just keep putting down one damn word after the other, as you hear them, as they come to you. You can either set brick as a laborer or as an artist. You can make the work a chore, or you can have a good time. You can do it the way you used to clear the dinner dishes when you were thirteen, or you can do it as a Japanese person would perform a tea ceremony, with a level of concentration and care in which you can lose yourself, and so in which you can find yourself.[35]

To care for someone who is depressed requires a level of concentration and care that can open up the caregiver to what it means to care in spite of feeling powerless. To offer care when seemingly unable to fix anything is a challenge for many caregivers. Some find it unbearable to become immersed in one's powerlessness to change the course of an illness, a depression. The challenge to the caregiver is to endure the powerlessness and to refuse to escape it.

Notes

Introduction

1. Sigmund Freud, "Mourning and Melancholia," in *Essential Papers on Depression*, ed. James C. Coyne (New York: New York University Press, 1986), 51.

2. Julia Kristeva, *The Black Sun: Depression and Melancholia*, trans. Leon S. Roudiez (New York: Columbia University Press, 1989), 5.

3. Robert Burton, *The Anatomy of Melancholy*, abr. and ed. by Joan K. Peters (New York: Frederick Ungar, 1979), 7.

4. Myrna M. Weissman and Gerald L. Klerman, "Sex Differences and the Epidemiology of Depression," *Archives of General Psychiatry* 34 (January 1977): 98–111. Many other studies replicate this data.

5. This argument has been well documented by Brant Wenegrat in *Illness and Power: Women's Mental Disorders and the Battle between the Sexes* (New York: New York University Press, 1995).

6. Ibid., 13.

7. "Setting a New Record for Women in the Senate," Congressional Facts and Figures, *The National Journal* 28, no. 23, June 8, 1996.

8. U.S. Bureau of the Census, *U.S. Population Estimate by Age, Sex, Race, and Hispanic Origin: 1989*, March 1990, table 1.

9. U.S. Bureau of the Census, Current Population Report, Series P-60, March 1994.

10. See Nancy Hartsock, *Money, Sex, and Power: Toward a Feminist Historical Materialism* (Boston: Northeastern University Press, 1985), 222–25; and Martha Ellen Stortz, *PastorPower* (Nashville: Abingdon Press, 1993).

11. Kristeva, *Black Sun*, 5.

Chapter 1.
Women, Depression, and Theology

1. This research is summarized in Ellen McGrath et al., eds., *Women and Depression: Risk Factors and Treatment Issues* (Washington, D.C.: American Psychological Association, 1990).

2. The one uniquely female biological vulnerability to depression is post-partum depression. See chapter 6, "Women's Bodies."

3. See G. W. Brown and T. O. Harris, *Social Origins of Depression: A Study of Psychiatric Disorder in Women* (London: Tavistock, 1978).

4. See Phyllis Chesler, *Women and Madness* (San Diego: Harcourt Brace Jovanovich, 1972); Kate Millett, *The Loony-Bin Trip* (New York: Simon & Schuster, 1990); Charlotte Perkins Gilman, *The Yellow Wallpaper* (New York: Feminist Press, 1990).

5. This lifespan model and the research cited here that supports it are found in Frederick K. Goodwin and Kay Redfield Jamison, *Manic-Depressive Illness* (New York: Oxford University Press, 1990), 405–7.

6. Ibid.

7. A correlation of an interpretation of the situation with an interpretation of Christian sources roughly describes the "revised correlation method" associated with theologian David Tracy. See his *Analogical Imagination: Christian Theology and the Culture of Pluralism* (New York: Crossroad, 1987).

8. It has been pointed out by a member of the scientific community that, if enough inert gas is diffused into a closed room, a person will suffocate. My intention is to emphasize the nonreactivity of inert gases, not their lethal potential.

9. Michel Foucault, *The Order of Things: An Archeology of the Human Sciences* (New York: Vintage Books, 1973), 312–18, 373, 386, quoted in Sharon D. Welch, *Communities of Resistance and Solidarity: A Feminist Theology of Liberation* (Maryknoll, N.Y.: Orbis Books, 1985), 12.

Chapter 2.
Cognitive Therapy

1. Other psychotherapeutic models are considered in the Appendix.

2. Freud, "Mourning and Melancholia," 48.

3. Ibid., 49.

4. Ibid., 53.

5. Sigmund Freud, *Civilization and Its Discontents*, trans. and ed. by James Strachey (New York: W. W. Norton & Co., Inc.: 1961).

6. Marie McGuire, *Men, Women, Passion, and Power: Gender Issues in Psychotherapy* (London: Routledge, 1995), 226.

7. See Howard Stone, *Brief Pastoral Counseling: Short-Term Approaches and Strategies* (Minneapolis: Fortress Press, 1994); and Brian Childs, *Short-Term Pastoral Counseling: A Guide* (Nashville: Abingdon Press, 1990). Also, James Lapsley advocates a cognitive-behavioral approach to pastoral care and counseling of the elderly in *Renewal in Late Life through Pastoral Counseling* (New York: Paulist Press, 1992).

8. See Aaron T. Beck, *Cognitive Therapy and the Emotional Disorders* (New York: Meridian Books, 1976); Aaron T. Beck et al., *Cognitive Therapy of Depression* (New York: Guilford Press, 1979).

9. Beck recognizes other factors in vulnerability to depression. He acknowledges that susceptibility to depression can be genetic, and that depressogenic assumptions

from childhood experiences can contribute to a vulnerability to depression. He also acknowledges that the precipitating factor is usually a loss. (Beck, *Cognitive Therapy and the Emotional Disorders*,102.) The most developed description of vulnerability factors in depression is his conceptualization of two personality types that respond with depression to two different kinds of losses. Personalities characterized by "social dependence" tend to become depressed with the loss or disruption of significant relationships. "Autonomous personalities" are triggered to depression by a perceived failure or inability to meet a goal, a loss of hope for achieving a desired end (Aaron T. Beck and Marjorie E. Weishaar, "Cognitive Therapy," in *Current Psychotherapies*, 4th ed., ed. Raymond J. Corsini and Danny Wedding [Itasca, Ill.: F. E. Peacock Publications, 1989], 294).

10. Beck et al., *Cognitive Therapy of Depression*, 14.

11. These questions are included on the *Dysfunctional Thought Record* distributed by the Center for Cognitive Therapy, Philadelphia.

12. Beck et al., *Cognitive Therapy of Depression*, 171.

13. Aaron Beck refers to a more elaborate record of thoughts and rational responses in his "Daily Record of Dysfunctional Thoughts" in Beck et al., *Cognitive Therapy of Depression*; David D. Burns refers to a "Daily Mood Log" in his *The Feeling Good Handbook* (New York: Penguin Books, 1990), 93.

14. Aaron T. Beck and Ruth L. Greenberg, "Cognitive Therapy with Depressed Women," *Women in Therapy: New Psychotherapies for a Changing Society* (New York: Brunner/Mazel, 1974), 130.

15. Janice Wood Wetzel, *Clinical Handbook of Depression* (New York: Gardner Press, 1984), 187.

16. Denise Davis and Christine Padesky, "Enhancing Cognitive Therapy with Women," in *Comprehensive Handbook of Cognitive Therapy*, ed. A. Freeman et al. (New York: Plenum Press, 1989), 539.

17. Ibid., 542–43.

18. Ibid., 550.

19. Miriam Greenspan, in *A New Approach to Women and Therapy* (New York: McGraw-Hill Book Co., 1983), speaks of de-selfing; Dana Crowley Jack, in *Silencing the Self: Women and Depression* (Cambridge, Mass.: Harvard University Press, 1991), refers to self silencing.

Chapter 3. Social Location

1. Julian of Norwich, *Revelations of Divine Love*, chap. xxvii.

2. Rebecca S. Chopp, *The Power to Speak: Feminism, Language, God* (New York: Crossroad, 1989), 103.

3. Ibid.

4. Greenspan, *A New Approach to Women and Therapy*, 193.

5. Ibid., 193–94.

6. McGrath et al., *Women and Depression*, 28.

7. Ibid.

8. Ibid., 33.

9. Barbara Jones Warren, "Depression in African-American Women," *Journal of Psychosocial Nursing* 32, no. 3 (1994): 31, citing D. R. Brown, "De-

pression among Blacks," S. E. Taylor, "The Mental Health Status of Black Americans: An Overview," in R. L. Braithwaite and S. E. Taylor, eds., *Health Issues in the Black Community* (San Francisco: Jossey-Bass, 1992), 20–34.

10. Ibid., 23.

11. Greenspan, *A New Approach to Women and Therapy*, 192.

12. C. H. Carrington, "Depression in Black Women: A Theoretical Appraisal," in *The Black Woman*, ed. La Frances Rodgers-Rose (Beverly Hills, Calif.: Sage Publications, 1980), 265–71; quoted in Warren, "Depression in African-American Women," 29–33.

13. I adapt this definition from Chris Weedon's statement: "The concept of a discursive field was produced by the French theorist, Michel Foucault, as part of an attempt to understand the relationship between language, social institutions, subjectivity, and power." Chris Weedon, *Feminist Practice and Poststructuralist Theory* (Oxford: Basil Blackwell, 1987), 35.

14. Michel Foucault, *Power/Knowledge: Selected Interviews and Other Writings, 1972–77* (New York: Pantheon, 1980), 131.

15. Ibid., 133.

16. Michel Foucault, *The Order of Things: An Archeology of the Human Sciences* (New York: Random House, 1970), xv.

17. Focault, *Power/Knowledge*, 142.

18. Ibid., 122.

19. Ibid., 132.

20. Ibid.

21. Ibid., 142.

22. Ibid.

23. Ibid.

24. Ibid., 116.

25. Ibid., 81.

26. Ibid., 81–82.

27. Ibid., 82.

28. Ibid.

29. Ibid.

30. Ibid.

31. Ibid.

32. Ibid.

33. Welch, *Communities of Resistance and Solidarity*, 15.

34. Ibid., quoting Mary Daly, *Beyond God the Father: Toward a Philosophy of Women's Liberation* (Boston: Beacon Press, 1973), 77.

35. Welch, *Communities of Resistance and Solidarity*, 19.

36. Welch cites a conversation with Lark D'Helen, fall 1982, in ibid., 15.

37. Ibid., 12, quoting Foucault, *The Order of Things*, 312–18, 373, 386.

38. Welch, *Communities of Resistance and Solidarity*, 52.

39. Ibid., 24, 25, quoting Dorothee Soelle, *Political Theology* (Philadelphia: Fortress Press, 1974), 76, 77.

40. Welch, *Communities of Resistance and Solidarity*, 25, 52. The similarities to American pragmatism cannot be overlooked. While Welch is drawing on liberationists and Foucault for her exploration of truth's "effects," the connections

between her thought and that of pragmatist William James warrant further exploration.

41. Mary Ballou and Nancy W. Gabalac, *A Feminist Position on Mental Health* (Springfield Ill.: Charles C Thomas, 1985), 90.

42. I am indebted to Elizabeth G. Maxwell for this insight.

43. Ballou and Gabalac, *A Feminist Position on Mental Health*, 99–100.

Chapter 4. Self

1. The potential inconsistencies between feminist psychologies' "self" and Foucault's "subject" merit a discussion that cannot be fully explored here, only briefly acknowledged. There are at least two ways feminist psychology is at odds with the features of Foucault I have presented here. First, most of them assume universal female psychic structures, such as, women are essentially relational (The Stone Center), women individuate in a certain way (Carol Gilligan), mothering is a key to understanding women (Nancy Chodorow), and so forth. These assumptions are implicit in the feminist psychologists cited here. Second, most of them speak of a true self that has been repressed or suppressed by patriarchy. The task of psychotherapy, then, is to help women discover and give voice to this true self.

Both the "universal female psyche" and the "true self" are clearly inconsistent with the Foucaultian "de-centered subject." For example, in "What is an Author?" Foucault speaks of the "death" or "disappearance" of the author, the end of the possibility of speaking of a pre-existing, originating self (Michel Foucault, "What is an Author?" in *The Foucault Reader*, ed. by Paul Rabinow [New York: Pantheon, 1984], 101ff., originally in *Textual Strategies: Perspectives in Post-structuralist Criticism*, ed. and trans. by Josue V. Harari [Ithaca, N.Y.: Cornell University, 1979], 141–60.) "Author" is rather a notion that performs a certain role: "The author function is therefore characteristic of the mode of existence, circulation, and function of certain discourses in a society" (Ibid., 108). The feminist psychologies presented here have not made the turn from pre-existing, originating self to the interplay of discourses, how they function, how they make possible certain subject positions. In Foucault the "individual" is not an originator of thought and action as feminist psychologies might assume, but a "node," a site of intersecting and competing discourses. Subject position is the focus in Foucault, not subject substance or content. The position that is possible, or impossible, in the fluctuating configurations of discourses is the concern, not a self that occupies that position.

A consideration of feminist psychology in a Foucaultian context raises certain questions. Is feminist psychology an attempt to give theoretical rigor to a discussion of the experience of white women in consciousness raising groups and self-discovery retreats, or white women in psychotherapy with a white feminist therapist? And in so doing is it universalizing experiences of white middle class women who have had the leisure to attend CR groups and retreats, and the funds for psychotherapy? Is it sufficiently conscious of the limits of its claims regarding female psychic structures? Furthermore, how has "feminist psychology" functioned as discourse to produce subjects? Who is elided by this discourse? These questions are rightly raised regarding feminist psychologies presented here. In spite of the inconsistencies with Foucault, and questions that he poses, I nevertheless maintain that "self" continues to be a useful category in a discussion of the care for depressed women, and for Foucaultian reasons. For a discussion of these reasons, see "The Socially Constructed Self" in this chapter. Also, see Jana Sawicki, *Disciplining Foucault: Feminism, Power, and the Body* (New York: Routledge, 1991), 95–109.

2. It is important to distinguish the loss of self as a *cause* of depression from the loss of self as a *symptom* of depression. For some feminist psychologists it seems that the cause of depression is continuous with its symptoms. For these theorists, depression is a silenced self, and it is a result of the active silencing of the self. They argue as though the analogy for depression is an empty glass that is empty because the water was poured out: depression is a silenced self because the self has been silenced. Yet the picture is more complicated than that. Depression is much more than a silencing of the self, or a loss of the self. The difficulties with concentration, sleep, appetite, and fatigue must also be accounted for. An empty-glass analogy does not work. Depression is more complex than the silencing of a self. It seems to be an illness where the cause, silencing the self, becomes a symptom, a silenced self, yet the cause triggers a host of accompanying symptoms as well. Certainly a silenced or lost self is a trigger for depression, and is a feature of the experience of depression, maybe the most prominent and painful one, yet there are other aspects as well.

3. I am indebted to Dana Crowley Jack for the language of "silencing the self," in *Silencing the Self*.

4. Donald Capps, personal communication.

5. The somewhat controllable self-ignoring can eventually become the uncontrollable self-eclipse that is depression. What began as active, willed self-silencing demonically assumes a life of its own and becomes much more than self-silencing, it becomes a self utterly silenced. Can one speak of "autoeclipse" in the way that one speaks of an "autoimmune" disease? Rather than the body's antibodies turning against it, the self turns against itself.

6. Harriet Goldhor Lerner, *Women in Therapy* (New York: Harper & Row, 1988), 201.

7. Ibid., 204.

8. Ibid., 201.

9. Jack, *Silencing the Self*, 32–33.

10. Mary McClintock Fulkerson has pointed out the parallels between this "self-policing" and Foucault's understanding of "discipline" rendering bodies "docile." [Michel Foucault, *Discipline and Punish: The Birth of the Prison* (New York: Vintage Books, 1979).]

11. Hope Landrine, "Clinical Implications of Cultural Differences," in *The Culture and Psychology Reader*, ed. Nancy Rule Goldberger and Jody Bennet Veroff (New York: New York University Press, 1995), 747.

12. Ibid., 751.

13. Nancy Hartsock, "Foucault on Power: A Theory for Women?" in *Fem-*

inism/Postmodernism, ed. Linda J. Nicholson (New York: Routledge & Kegan Paul, 1990), 163.

14. Unfortunately, Foucault's zeal in debunking the notion of the unified, originating self has been read as a claim that individuals do not exist at all. In fact, he was attempting to call our attention to the profound limits placed by our social, cultural, political, economic positioning, and that we are not the rational, freely choosing selves we might think we are. He was discrediting claims to make universal truth about anything, such as "essential humanity" or "womanness," not suggesting that human beings or women do not exist. Jana Sawicki quotes Ian Hacking: "Foucault said the concept of Man is a fraud, not that you and I are nothing." (Ian Hacking, "The Archeology of Foucault," in *Foucault: A Critical Reader*, ed. David Couzens Hoy, [London: Basil Blackwell, 1986], 39; quoted in Jana Sawicki, "Feminism and the Power of Foucauldian Discourse," in *After Foucault: Humanistic Knowledge, Postmodern Challenges*, ed. Jonathan Arac [New Brunswick: Rutgers, 1986], 174.) Therefore, it is important not to read Foucault as suggesting that living human beings are an illusion or a fantasy, a suggestion that is not only absurd but not useful for those interested in offering care.

15. Toril Moi, "Introduction," in *The Kristeva Reader*, ed. Toril Moi (New York: Columbia University Press, 1986), 15.

16. Michel Foucault, "The Subject and Power," in *Michel Foucault: Beyond Structuralism and Hermeneutics*, Hubert Dreyfus, Paul Rabinow (Chicago: University of Chicago Press, 1982), 208.

17. Julia Kristeva, *In the Beginning Was Love: Psychoanalysis and Faith*, trans. Arthur Goldhammer (New York: Columbia University Press, 1987), 9.

18. Ibid.

19. Ibid., 14.

20. Moi, *Kristeva Reader*, 13.

21. Ibid., 13–14.

22. Dale B. Martin, personal communication.

23. Sylvia Plath, *The Bell Jar* (New York: Harper & Row, 1961).

24. Carrie Doehring has also made rich use of literature for pastoral theology in *Taking Care: Monitoring Power Dynamics and Relational Boundaries in Pastoral Care and Counseling* (Nashville: Abingdon Press, 1995).

25. Plath, *The Bell Jar*, 8, 14.

26. Ibid., 15.

27. Ibid., 11.

28. Ibid., 79.

29. Ibid., 8.

30. Ibid., 15.

31. Ibid., 16.

32. Ibid., 17.

33. Ibid.

34. Ibid.

35. Ibid., 20.

36. Ibid., 21.

37. Ibid., 5.

38. Ibid., 23.
39. Ibid., 24.
40. Ibid., 152.
41. Ibid.
42. Ibid.
43. Ibid., 176.
44. Ibid., 197.

Chapter 5. Relationship

1. Catherine Keller, *From a Broken Web: Separation, Sexism, and Self* (Boston: Beacon Press, 1986), 3; second emphasis mine.

2. There is debate among feminists about whether women are relational by nature or by nurture. I want to make it clear that I am not making the essentialist claim that women are by nature more oriented toward relationship than men, that there is something inherent in womanness that is relational. At this point, I want to leave the question open, and simply state that women *tend* to be more relationship-oriented than men, for whatever reason.

3. Carol Gilligan, *Making Connections: The Relational Worlds of Adolescent Girls at Emma Willard School* (Cambridge, Mass.: Harvard University Press, 1990).

4. McGrath et al., *Women and Depression*, 17.

5. Lerner, *Women in Therapy*, 224.

6. Ibid.

7. Jack, *Silencing the Self*, 27.

8. Elizabeth G. Maxwell, personal communication.

9. Irene Goldenberg, Herberg Goldenberg, *Family Therapy: An Overview, Second Edition* (Pacific Grove, Calif.: Brooks/Cole Publishing Co., 1985), 237–8.

10. Ilene J. Philipson, *On the Shoulders of Women: The Feminization of Psychotherapy* (New York: Guilford, 1993), 98, summarizing the argument of T. Goodrich, C. Rampage, B. Ellman, *Feminist Family Therapy: A Casebook* (New York: Norton, 1988).

11. Rachel Hare-Mustin, "The Problem of Gender in Family Therapy Theory," in Monica McGoldrick, Carol Anderson, Froma Walsh, eds., *Women in Families: A Framework for Family Therapy* (New York: W. W. Norton, 1989), 66.

12. Ballou and Gabalac, *Feminist Position on Mental Health*. I am indebted to Christie Cozad Neuger for the referral to this useful resource. She includes this selection from the Ballou and Gabalac book in her "Women and Depression: Lives at Risk", in Glaz and Moessner, *Women in Travail*, 158.

13. See Neuger, "Women's Depression," 159.

14. We are indebted to Nelle Morton for the phrase "hearing into speech." This has been an enduring way of expressing the way women empower one another through the hearing and telling of stories. Morton uses this phrase in *The Journey Is Home* (Boston: Beacon Press, 1985).

15. Carolyn G. Heilbrun, *Writing a Woman's Life* (New York: Ballantine Books, 1988), 11.

16. Ibid., 17.

17. I am indebted to Richard Hays for the notion of "echoes of scripture." *Echoes of Scripture in the Letters of Paul* (New Haven, Conn.: Yale University Press, 1989).

18. Stanley Fish refers to "interpretive communities" that "are made up of those who share interpretive strategies not for reading (in the conventional sense) but for writing texts, for constituting their properties and assigning their intentions." In these communities, "meanings are not extracted but made not by encoded forms but by interpretive strategies that call forms into being" (Stanley E. Fish, "Interpreting the *Valorium*," in *Reader-Response Criticism: From Formalism to Post-Structuralism*, ed. Jane P. Tompkins [Baltimore: Johns Hopkins University Press, 1980], 182–83). It is such a community that I refer to as a "reading community."

19. I am indebted to Walter Wink for this insight.

20. Elizabeth A. Johnson, *She Who Is: The Mystery of God in Feminist Theological Discourse* (New York: Crossroad, 1995), 66.

21. Ibid.

22. Ibid., 67.

Chapter 6.
Women's Bodies

1. Margaret Atwood, "The Female Body," in *Minding the Body: Women Writers on Body and Soul*, ed. Patricia Foster (New York: Doubleday, 1994), 91.

2. Greenspan, *A New Approach to Women and Therapy*, 161ff.

3. Ibid., 166.

4. I am indebted to Martha Ellen Stortz for this typology of power as commodity, relationship, and capacity, in *PastorPower*.

5. Gloria Anzaldúa, "Speaking in Tongues: A Letter to 3rd World Women Writers," in *This Bridge Called My Back: Writings by Radical Women of Color*, ed. Cherríe Moraga and Gloria Anzaldua (Watertown, Mass.: Persephone, 1981), 169. Originally written for *Words in Our Pockets* (San Francisco: Bootlegger), the Feminist Writers' Guild handbook.

6. Cheryl Townsend Gilkes, "The 'Loves' and 'Troubles' of African-American Women's Bodies: The Womanist Challenge to Cultural Humiliation and Community Ambivalence," in *A Troubling in My Soul: Womanist Perspectives on Evil and Suffering*, ed. Emilie M. Townes (Maryknoll, N.Y.: Orbis Books, 1993), 246.

7. Patricia Hill Collins, *Black Feminist Thought: Knowledge, Consciousness, and the Politics of Empowerment* (New York: Unwin Hyman, 1990), 72.

8. Ibid., 74.

9. Ibid., 76–77.

10. Ibid., 78.

11. Sylvia Plath, *The Journals of Sylvia Plath*, ed. Frances McCullough (New York: Dial Press, 1982), 60–61.

12. Pam Houston, "Out of Habit, I Start Apologizing," in *Minding the Body*, ed. Patricia Foster, 148.

13. Ibid., 149.

14. Ibid., 149–50.

15. Bureau of Justice Statistics, "Report to the Nation on Crime and Justice" (Washington D.C.: Office of Justice Program, U.S. Department of Justice, October 1983).

16. Uniform Crime Reports, Federal Bureau of Investigation, 1991.

17. Barbara Hart, Remarks to the Task Force on Child Abuse and Neglect (April 1992).

18. Lenore E. Walker, *The Battered Woman* (San Francisco: Harper & Row, 1979).

19. McGrath et al, *Women and Depression*, 13–14.

20. Ibid., 9–10.

21. Ibid., 10.

22. Ibid., 11.

23. Ibid., 11–12.

24. Ibid., 12.

25. Christie Neuger, "Women's Depression: Lives at Risk," in *Women in Travail and Transition: A New Pastoral Care*, Maxine Glaz and Jeanne Stevenson Moessner, eds. (Minneapolis: Fortress, 1991), 149.

26. Rosemary Radford Ruether, "Motherearth and the Megamachine: A Theology of Liberation in a Feminine, Somatic, and Ecological Perspective," in *Womanspirit Rising: A Feminist Reader in Religion*, ed. Carol Christ and Judith Plaskow (San Francisco: Harper & Row, 1979), 43ff.

27. Michel Foucault, "Nietzsche, Genealogy, History," in *The Foucault Reader*, ed. Paul Rabinow (New York: Pantheon Books, 1984), 83; emphasis mine.

28. Ibid., 87.

29. Michel Foucault, *Discipline and Punish: The Birth of the Prison* (New York: Vintage Books, 1979), 24.

30. Ibid., 25.

31. Ibid., 26.

32. Susan Bordo, "Anorexia Nervosa: Psychopathology as the Crystallization of Culture," in *Feminism & Focault: Reflections on Resistance*, Irene Diamond and Lee Quinby, eds. (Boston: Northeastern University Press, 1988), 87ff.

33. Robert McAfee Brown, *Elie Wiesel: Messenger to All Humanity* (Notre Dame, Ind.: Notre Dame University Press, 1983).

34. See James Nelson, *Embodiment: An Approach to Sexuality and Christian Theology* (Minneapolis: Augsburg Publishing House, 1978).

Chapter 7. Anger

1. For a helpful exploration of anger see the recent work of pastoral theologian Carroll Saussy in *The Gift of Anger: A Call to Faithful Action* (Louisville, Ky.: Westminster John Knox Press, 1995).

2. D. G. Bagby, *Dictionary of Pastoral Care and Counseling*, ed. Rodney J. Hunter et al. (Nashville: Abingdon Press, 1990), 40.

3. Freud, "Mourning and Melancholia," 54.

4. Ibid., 48.

5. Ibid., 49.

6. Ibid., 53.

7. Beverly Wildung Harrison, "The Power of Anger in the Work of Love," in *Making the Connections: Essays in Feminist Social Ethics*, ed. Carol S. Robb (Boston: Beacon Press, 1985), 14.

8. Ibid.

9. Ibid.

10. Audre Lorde, *Sister/Outsider: Essays and Speeches* (Freedom, Calif.: Crossing Press, 1984), 124.

11. Lerner, *Women in Therapy*, 222.

12. Ibid.; emphasis mine.

13. Carol Tavris, *Anger: The Misunderstood Emotion* (New York: Simon & Schuster, 1982), 132.

14. Greenspan, *A New Approach to Women and Therapy*, 301; emphasis mine.

15. Ibid., 303.

16. Ibid., 305.

17. Ibid., 314.

18. Ibid.

19. See David Burns, *Feeling Good: The New Mood Therapy* (New York: Signet Books, 1980), 175–77.

20. Lorde, *Sister/Outsider*, 127.

21. Comments by Nancy Ramsay contributed to this insight in a workshop led by Carroll Saussy at the 1996 meeting of the Society for Pastoral Theology in Denver, Colorado.

22. Andrew D. Lester, *Coping with Your Anger: A Christian Guide* (Philadelphia: Westminster Press, 1983), 11.

23. Ibid., 12.

24. Ibid., 14.

25. Harrison, "The Power of Anger in the Work of Love," 15.

26. Johnson, *She Who Is*, 257.

27. Ibid., 258.

28. Ibid.; emphasis mine.

29. Greenspan, *A New Approach to Women and Therapy*, 195.

30. Ibid., 196.

31. Ibid.

32. J. C. Wynn, *Family Therapy in Pastoral Ministry: Counseling for the Nineties* (San Francisco: HarperCollins, 1982), 41–42.

Chapter 8. Hope

1. "Abide with Me," in *The Hymnbook* (Richmond: Presbyterian Church in the United States, 1955), 64.

2. "Hark, What a Sound," in *The Hymnbook*, 150.

3. William Styron, *Darkness Visible: A Memoir of Madness* (New York: Random House, 1990), 63.

4. Donald Capps, *Agents of Hope: A Pastoral Psychology* (Minneapolis: Fortress Press, 1995), 166.

5. Ibid., 164.

6. Ibid., quoting Richard Bandler and John Brinder, *Reframing: Neuro-Linguistic Programming and the Transformation of Meaning* (Moab, Utah: Real People Press, 1982), 1.

7. Capps, *Agents of Hope*, 165.

8. Capps takes this method from Ben Furman and Tapani Ahola, *Solution Talk: Healing Therapeutic Conversations* (New York: W. W. Norton & Co., 1992), 91–106.

9. Capps, *Agents of Hope*, 169.

10. Ibid., 170.

11. Ibid., 175.

12. Ibid.

13. Capps takes this phrase from Mordechai Rotenberg, "The 'Midrash' and Biographical Rehabilitation," *Journal for the Scientific Study of Religion* 25 (1986): 41–55.

14. Capps, *Agents of Hope*, 175.

15. Ibid.

16. Andrew D. Lester, *Hope in Pastoral Care and Counseling* (Louisville, Ky.: Westminster John Knox Press, 1995), 109ff.

17. Ibid., 139.

18. Ibid., 144.

19. Ibid., 145.

20. Ibid.

21. Ibid.

22. Chopp, *The Power to Speak*, 102; emphasis mine.

23. Ibid., 103; emphasis mine.

24. Sharon Welch, *A Feminist Ethic of Risk* (Minneapolis: Fortress Press, 1989), 172.

25. Ibid., quoting Carter Heyward, *Our Passion for Justice: Images of Power, Sexuality, and Liberation* (New York: Pilgrim Press, 1984); emphasis mine.

26. Ibid., 173.

27. Ibid., 177.

28. Ibid., 177–178.

29. Ibid., 179.

30. Anne Lamott, *Bird by Bird: Some Instructions on Writing and Life* (New York: Pantheon Books, 1994), 18–19.

31. Capps, *Agents of Hope*, 148–151.

32. Adrienne Rich, *The Fact of a Doorframe: Poems Selected and New, 1950–1984* (New York: W. W. Norton & Co., 1984), 273–74; quoted in Capps, *Agents of Hope*, 148.

33. Lamott, *Bird by Bird*, xxiii.

34. Gloria Naylor, *The Women of Brewster Place* (New York: Penguin Books, 1980), 102–3.

35. Lamott, *Bird by Bird*.

Index